D0599018

WRITING
DRAMATIC
NONFICTION

Books by William Noble

Three Rules for Writing a Novel
        Forest Dale, Vermont, 1997

The Complete Guide to Writers' Conferences and Workshops,
        Forest Dale, Vermont, 1995

Show, Don't Tell, Middlebury, Vermont, 1991

Bookbanning in America, Middlebury, Vermont, 1990

Make That Scene, Middlebury, Vermont, 1988

"Shut Up!" He Explained, Middlebury, Vermont, 1987

Books with June Noble

Steal This Plot, Middlebury, Vermont, 1985

The Psychiatric Fix, New York, 1981

The Private Me, New York, 1980

How to Live With Other People's Children, New York, 1978

The Custody Trap, New York, 1975

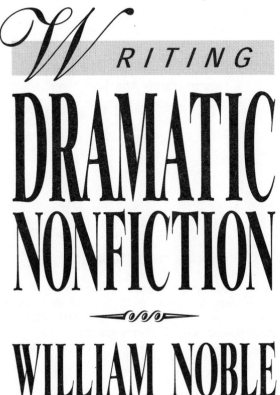

WRITING

DRAMATIC NONFICTION

WILLIAM NOBLE

PAUL S. ERIKSSON, *PUBLISHER*
FOREST DALE, VERMONT

For my lovely Angela

—⚬⚬⚬—

5 4 3 2 1

Library of Congress Cataloging-in-Publication Data

Noble, William.
    Writing dramatic nonfiction / by William Noble.
        p. cm.
    Includes bibliographical references and index.
    ISBN 0-8397-8645-X (cloth)
        1. Authorship. I. Title.

PN187 .N63 2000
808'.02--dc21

00-035342

Design by Eugenie S. Delaney

Contents

—∞∞∞—

Preface

It's said often enough. Every writer claims there's a book he or she has always wanted to write, and, cliché or not, this book represents that target for me. I've long felt nonfiction is where the literary action is because fact-based writing is still in the developing stage and offers exciting challenges for writers.

What's happened, particularly since the 1960s, is that writers have discovered what makes fiction a powerful art form is adaptable to nonfiction. The finished product can rhapsodize and offend and memorialize in the same way as fiction, often using the same or similar dramatic technique. Some bemoan this consequence, citing it as a blurring of the line between fiction and nonfiction. Confusing and ultimately unproductive, they say, how will we know what's fact and what's not?

The answer, of course, lies in the writer's sense of duty and responsibility to the readers. He or she should make known any license taken with facts, and , if possible, offer a solid explanation about what was done. Norman Mailer did it with *The Executioner's Song,* his saga about the life and death of double-murderer Gary Gilmore. Mailer calls it a factual account, a true life story but then he adds: "This does not mean it has come a great deal closer to the truth than the recollections of the witnesses . . . ." He's telling us where he got his information, but he's also advising that he will be writing a "story," and that means he'll be taking license.

In recent years nonfiction forms have undergone drama-development makeover: from personal essay to memoir to restaurant review to travel article to personality profile to feature article to biography, even to science reporting, and the result has been exciting and thought-provoking. If a staid piece of conventional reporting can be juiced up with fiction devices such as extended dialogue or flashbacks and the essential factual basis remain untouched, why not offer readers a "story" instead of a "report"? Why not entertain readers and gather them inside the story rather than bombard them from afar?

This is what the nonfiction resurgence has meant, and because we're still in the early stages an entire art form is evolving. Good nonfiction writing today can mean the simplest adjustment. Author Tim Cahill puts it well: A traditional journalist would ask, "What did you see?" But the untraditional journalist would ask: "How did you feel about what you were seeing? What was happening inside you at that moment?" In this dichotomy is the essence of change that we're now seeing. When we explore the writer's personal reactions to the story, we've come a long way from strict, objective just-the-facts journalism. And at the same time we've established the foundation for artistic expression because we're now dealing in *impressions*, and that develops meaning and substance and truth—all of them the end product of artistic development.

An underlying assumption with this book is that nonfiction, just as fiction, can rise to the level of art. It requires hard work on the writer's part and an understanding of the demands artistic expression makes. It isn't enough simply to tell a good story, not when the writer seeks to turn the work into art. Beautiful expression is needed, impressionistic awareness and application are needed, and in the end the work must shed light on our nature as human beings. Art is the universal language of creativity, and in the following pages, it will be seen that the nonfiction writer can be equally as creative as the fiction writer. When that creativity is turned to storytelling, it doesn't matter whether the story is actual or imagined. The same dramatic techniques are available to nonfiction and fiction writer alike, and the opportunity to develop artistic expression exists at the core of any writer's true ethic.

ART ONE

The Art
of Nonfiction

The Art of Nonfiction

———☙☙☙———

The late novelist, John Gardner, once wrote: "Art depends heavily on feeling, intuition, taste . . . " and he decried applying rules to what he conceived as pure, truthful spontaneity. Art was anything that worked, and rules limited and contaminated the artist. Gardner was speaking of fiction, but his words ring with resonance for nonfiction, too. The writer as artist isn't limited to novelists and poets; there are essayists and memoirists and historians and journalists and scientists — nonfiction writers all — who have taken us inside their worlds and dazzled us with their prose and their artistry.

Where the fiction writer asks, How *might* this have happened? the nonfiction writer asks, How *did* this happen?. Yet art and artistry can flower for both. Fact-based writing can reach creative levels just as fiction writing does, and in the hands of an accomplished nonfiction writer imaginative use of facts can be transformed and become art.

John Gardner spoke of feeling, intuition and taste, and there's little dispute that when applied to fiction these characteristics are there. Look no further than Ernest Hemingway's

The Old Man and the Sea where his protagonist, Santiago, the old fisherman, alternately rhapsodizes about and bemoans his lot as he lands the huge fish that could bring him material salvation. What feelings are there for us in Hemingway's portrayal? Sadness, concern, hope, fear, support? Weave this with intuitive empathy for Santiago's doomed struggle because of the heroic possibilities that could emerge. It's as when a subdued piece of music rises inexorably to crescendo, widening and deepening as it goes.

But the story could still fail as art if Hemingway applied tasteless effects such an unsympathetic ending or a coarse, vulgar story mood. It's the author's sense of taste, Gardner says, that confirms the presence of art, and when it isn't there, the written product fails. Art, he insists, must begin with the writer's attitude, an awareness of something new, something different. "Restating old truths" is what he says the artist must seek to do, "adapting them to the age, applying them in ways they were never before applied, stirring up emotions by the inherent power of narrative, visual image or music . . . ."

What Gardner says about fiction writing is equally appropriate to nonfiction. Imagine an apple ready for plucking from the artistry tree: the important thing isn't who does the plucking but how it's plucked. That's how art develops. Fiction or nonfiction doesn't matter, creative development does, and out of creativity comes artistry.

Reynolds Price, novelist and poet, sees creativity — even artistry — in that most mundane of events — the dreams we experience each night. For him creativity through dreaming is a spark we might bring to routine events as well as extraordinary ones. "Dreams are obviously the art of the artless," he writes. "I mean people who don't write poetry, choreograph, paint pictures, whatever, do in fact, every night when they're asleep, construct works of art in their heads."

If everyone possesses artistry, how can we limit the ability to express art to only a special few? Must all of us be fiction writers in order to qualify as artists? If we dream and create, why can't it be based upon fact and become nonfiction? Why can't we apply our creative talents, dramatize a series of facts, and have it become art?

Take a look at Richard Seltzer's *Mortal Lessons*. Seltzer, a surgeon, offers essays and narrative description on elements of his work, and he brings artistic flair and creative dimension to what in most hands would be matter-of-fact exposition. He negotiates the key test for any artist — taking the mundane and transforming it into something special. He does this by employing a classic artist's technique: emphasizing the aesthetic, appealing to the reader's aesthetic sensibilities. Here, he writes about peering into the cavity of the human abdomen:

"Such a primitive place. One expects to find drawings of buffalo on the walls. The sense of trespassing is keener now, heightened by the world's light illuminating the organs, their secret colors revealed — maroon and salmon and yellow. The vista is secretly vulnerable at this moment, a kind of welcoming. An arc of the liver shines high and on the right, like a dark sun . . ."

Can anyone imagine a less beautiful place than the inside of a stomach? Yuk!

But note how Seltzer handles it: his tone is respectful, even loving; he calls himself a trespasser; he calls the scene "sweetly vulnerable," and we sense his empathy for the patient and the patient's organs. He gives us the colors of the internal organs, not in stark description (such as "blood red" or "dark, ominous blue") but in softer colorings: "maroon and salmon and yellow," calling them "secret" colors, and we find the imagery more acceptable. He gives us an aesthetic vision of the liver, its "arc" and we sense it's much more to him than a simple organ. Arc, after all, has poetic connotation. In Chaucer's *Man of Law's Tale* (prologue) we see:

The brighte sonne
The *arc* of his artificial day
hath ronne . . .

Seltzer's use of such words and phrases provides a foundation for aesthetic wanderings even with the most prosaic subjects . . . such as the inside of the stomach. The important thing to remember is that using such references not only enlivens the nonfiction prose but if developed properly can turn it into art.

Think for a moment about the kind of words that could accomplish this: poetic words, items of beauty and joy, solid references to colors, transcendent feelings, harmony. Words and phrases like these:

starry skies
lord of far horizons
autumn sunsets
partaken bliss
lily among thorns
random ebullience
perfumed sea
angel love

Each of these appears in poetic form somewhere, and clearly they offer artistic possibilities. But suppose we take Seltzer's view of the open abdomen and use a couple of the above phrases:

"The organs, now, illuminated as golden autumn sunset, sharing partaken bliss with a perfumed sea of soft, worldly light . . ."

It's nonfiction, to be sure, but it's aesthetically so, and doesn't that make it appealing?

The poetry connection can be useful when we're developing art with nonfiction. There's no reason why a writer can't think in poetic terms even as he or she produces nonfiction. Aesthetics aside, the very nature of poetry is an appeal to artistry because it's conceptual and strives to influence taste and beauty. Poetic technique can be used to buttress nonfiction, and when it's done well, the aesthetics stand out.

See how Diane Ackerman does it with her *The Rarest of the Rare,* a look at endangered species and what is being done to help them. She is a scientist, a Ph.D., and one might expect complicated, dry explanation in her writing. Not so . . . and in fact her prose rings with poetic technique and aesthetic reference. Here she is after studying the short-tailed albatross at their sole habitat, an island about 500 miles south of Tokyo. She observes a lone albatross, as the boat pulls away from the island:

"For some time we stand in the glow of the setting sun and watch the albatross cartwheel over the waves, changing from white when it's framed by dark water to black when it's framed by the

7

paler sky. Positive and negative, it drives from
the transparent air down to the thick gelid water
and up again, lacing the sea and sky together with
its swooping flight.

Note the contrasting effects here: black and white, sea
and sky, positive and negative, transparent and gelid, each a
way of establishing dimension and substance. But anyone
can throw in contrast words and phrases; what makes this art
is how she surrounds the words with aesthetic appeal: white
is "framed by the darker water," black is "framed by the paler
sky." The bird is "lacing the sea and sky together," its flight
"swooping." "Lacing" and "swooping" are poetic words
because they call up aesthetics, something lovely and free and
graceful. "Positive and negative" stand out there by themselves, seemingly without aesthetic trappings. But note to
what they refer: the white and black that are "framed . . . " and
so they take their effect from these aesthetic offerings. It's like
John Keats' phrase from *Ode On a Grecian Urn*: "Beauty is
truth, truth beauty . . ."; we may not be able to compose it as
well as Keats, but we can certainly write about beauty to
imply its purity (which is what Keats was after), and our words
will be buttressed by Keats' classic formulation. Just as a
memorable sunset can be heightened by the whispy white
appearance of the early moon, our sense and application of
aesthetics grows because of John Keats.

Beauty is what we're after, and if we consult a thesaurus
(Roget's 1971 edition will do) we'll see certain synonyms: ". . .
elegance, grace . . . symmetry . . . comeliness, fairness . . . pul-
chritude, polish, gloss . . . bloom, brilliancy, radiance, splen-
dor, gorgeousness, magnificence . . . ." If our writing can
employ one or more of these effects, then the medium of the

writing — nonfiction or fiction — doesn't matter. The real question is how we do it (remember the example of the plucked apple?), and the answer lies partly in developing poetic instincts and practices, in seeking an aesthetic rendering, as Diane Ackerman does, and applying them to our nonfiction.

Watch the way Lewis Thomas does it with his book *The Lives of A Cell,* a title that might not catch our interest unless we were into biology as he is. We'd be foolish to turn away, however, because as Diane Ackerman does, Thomas takes scientific exposition and renders it art-like by highlighting those effects that embrace art. Where Ackerman uses poetic contrast, Thomas portrays nature, or a portion thereof, as an artistic vehicle, offering a viewpoint that is based on science but is portrayed as art. He provides clear information — facts, facts, facts! — but note how it comes over. He speaks of the need for organisms to make music, to be "fully orchestrated," so we might become aware of the "counterpoint, the balances of tones and timbres and harmonies, the sonorities." He mentions the recorded songs of the humpback whale, brimming with "tensions and resolutions, ambiguities and allusions" and comprising a small part of nature's music. He goes on:

> "If . . . [we] could discern the descants of sea birds,
> the rhythmic timpani of schools of mollusks, or
> even the distant harmonies of midges hanging
> over meadows in the sun, the combined sound
> might lift us off our feet . . . "

What Lewis Thomas does is develop artistry by analogy to a classic art form — orchestration and music. Who could ever imagine that the strange, weird noises we hear in the garden or the seemingly unconnected sounds that come to us out of the night air could form a musical panoply for this biologist? But the fact that he can see art in what most of us ignore or find uninspiring is exactly why his thoughts and views are memorable. He has culled art out of the hard rock of fact, and he has made it plain that the mine of art and artistry is clearly untapped. Suppose we wanted to follow his example, how would we do it?

It's a three-step process: first, we pick an art form — music, dance, sculpture, painting, etc.; second, we pick out those characteristics of our nonfiction subject that might provide artistic possibilities (for example, if we write about marble quarries, we might highlight the sculpted residue of pit walls after the quarry is abandoned); third, we inject the characteristics with aesthetic expression (such as the exuberant beauty of the shapes and figures remaining on the walls, even as the quarry stands lifeless).

For example, we could write of "the silvery madonna at the crest of a velvety round outcropping . . . " or the "shadowed lily with its broken petals" and be speaking about sculpted portions of the abandoned pit. We add aesthetics, and what do we get? A touch of art with our nonfiction.

But art is much more than aesthetics, and when we write, we have other techniques available. One of the more interesting, though demanding, to consider, is the use of "neologisms," or the development of new words and phrases — in effect, to create something not seen before. Since the basis of art is creativity, the more inventive we are with words and/or word sounds, the more attention we'll attract. I recall the time a writer friend and I were driving along a rural road in deep, dense fog. We tried to keep our left wheel on the edge of the white line that bisected the road, and after about an hour of arduous driving, he let out a breath and said, "You ever wonder who invented the white line and how many lives it saved?"

The inventor of the white line probably couldn't be traced, but the significance of the invention is key because it provides substance and dimension (greater usage, greater safety) to the driving experience . . . in the same way neologisms add to the text in which they appear. Neologisms offer creativity by their very nature and become art when the words conjure images and/or sounds for the reader. BANG! . . . we read, and our inner senses are jarred because we conjure unpleasant images. If a neologism accomplishes the same thing, pleasant or unpleasant, it's artistry because the entire image has been "created" in a way not done before. What the neologism has done is take the mundane, the usual, and make it something special.

For example, let's look at the sport of baseball and at Roger Angell who has spent many years writing about it. Most of us pooh-pooh the idea there could be art arising out of sports writing, that art is the antithesis of sweaty people chasing a ball or swinging a club or moving their arms and legs as fast as they can. "Sport is sport, art is art" is the way a journalist friend once put it, and for him the separation was irretrievable.

But then there's Roger Angell, and in his approach to baseball he strives for artistry. One way he does it is to offer neologisms because they create a sense, a mood that transcends the conventional and the uninspired. Here's how he writes about an organ at New York's Yankee Stadium that bursts into riffs and trills even when play stops for only a few seconds. The "almost creaseless commentary abrades the fabric of the game and the soul of the watching fan," he states, and then he mimics the electronic monster. " . . . *Buh* da-da-da-da! *Buh* da-da-da-da! *Buh* da-da! *BUH* da-da-da-da-da-da! (Theme from "Gaite Parisienne" here repeated in read up tempo.) Pause. 'Tah-tah-tah TAHHH' (Beethoven's Fifth, opening theme.) Pause. 'Beedle-di-deet, dah-dah-dah-deet! Beedle-di-tweet, dah-dah-dah-tweet!' (Theme from 'Dardenella,' for seven seconds.) Pause . . ."

He carries this on for another full paragraph, showing how the organ mimics sound-bites from films such as "Jaws," musical themes such as the Colonel Bogey March, commercial jingles from well-known products and so on. All of this plays on the reader's ear, showing the irritating, puerile intrusions which, in turn, make the reader appreciate even more what Roger Angell is trying to say.

The idea of reducing sound effects to words is not new (see Tom Wolfe's work in the 1960s especially), but the precise recitation of these sounds is. Who has ever tried to mimic a blasting Wurlitzer, who has ever applied such critique to a mood-setter at a sporting event?

This entire effect is a neologism, and in its application it becomes art — not because it's beautiful (it's not!), but because it heightens our conceptual instincts and provides us with greater understanding and appreciation than if the word-sounds had not been there.

Suppose Roger Angell had written:

"The huge organ destroys my interest in
the game because it's too loud, interrupts
the flow and sounds so childish . . ."

Same thoughts, same feelings but what a difference! The second is explanation, the first is art.

Neologisms don't have to be unique phrases or creative recitations of sounds. To acquire a label as neologism, nonfiction expression must be new, different, imaginative!

Even a single word will do.

Something that takes expression from pedestrian comfort and shoots it to rarefied uniqueness, that offers conceptual purity along with never-before experienced understanding.

Such as this passage from surgeon Richard Seltzer's description of our nails in his *Mortal Lessons:*

> "One parts with the nails only under political
> duress and in great pain. Long since having
> retired their acquisitive and protective functions,
> they are more like sweet hooflets of a yearling
> than the talons of a hawk . . ."

If "hooflets" isn't a neologism, it's as close to one as we're likely to get. Note what he has done here: he has taken a perfectly good noun (hoof) and diminished it by adding "let," thus providing us with a new word and a new meaning:

> *hooflet:* curved covering of horn protecting
> the open foot tissue of a young, small mammal . . .

It's not a hoof, it's a "hooflet," thus offering a new word with limited application: young, small mammal (a "yearling") with "hooflets," not hoofs.

A single new word like this wouldn't carry an entire passage to artistic heights without substantially more. But what it shows is that with nonfiction just as with fiction there is a place for neologisms and that artistry thrives on such creative uses of new word forms. There is no automatic formula for creating and developing neologisms, but we should be alert to the opportunity to present them, regardless of whether we're writing biography, memoir, narrative history, journalistic description or any of the other nonfiction forms. The important thing to realize is that we shouldn't avoid them because they may be new, untried or even strange-looking. Art, after all, is a response to conventional attitudes, and art's initial impact depends to a great extent on how unusual, creative and innovative it is. If a piece of work mirrors convention and usual scenes, what we have is re-creation, not creative development. It is the unusual, the offbeat, the strange, the new that have a better chance to become art.

The one thing about art there's no dispute over is that we gauge it by its effect upon us. And how do we measure this effect? By what goes through our minds, by what pictures or images blossom there. Suppose we come across the following:

> "It's hard to find a more dangerous job than
> venturing onto the whaleback during a storm
> to do a little carpentry. On land the 100-knot
> wind reduces people to a crawl; at sea it knocks
> you flat. The decks are awash, the boat is
> rolling, the spray is raking you like grapeshot . . ."

Can we imagine this scene: a howling storm at sea, trying to fix something outside on deck? The imagery is clear-cut and fearsome, the threat to life unvarnished, and our minds fill with the events and the precarious circumstances.

But is is art? The passage is from Junger's *The Perfect Storm,* an arresting story about fishermen who make their living thousands of miles from home, sometimes in most frightening weather conditions. If we look at art as something that, among other things, projects imagery into our minds, then this book certainly qualifies because chapter after chapter details life and death under the severest circumstances. Descriptions abound: far, far from home, monstrous seas, diabolically dangerous storm patterns, frightful winds, broken shipboard equipment, loss of life, panic, heroism . . . .

Art, we've seen, is the representation of something out of the ordinary, something conceptual, something that makes us think and/or feel. Does this book do that?

Probably so, and once again we have a piece of nonfiction that rises to an artistic level. The problem, of course, is that it is such a good story that it has become so popular, its image-making so pervasive, there are those who feel it shouldn't occupy that rarefied place where art resides.

But who says art has to be so exclusive it can't be enjoyed by many, many people, that it has to have a narrow application? If the work qualifies because of intrinsic value and worth, then it's artistry no matter how broad its appeal.

Imagery is one imporant thing art seeks to project, and in the best of circumstances we carry that imagery with us when we come upon it. Good poetry provides consistent, affecting imagery, and most of us sense our minds open and absorb images the poet has offered. For example, in this passage from Alfred Lord Tennyson's *Locksley Hall* note the image of a woman's face:

> "On her pallid cheek and forehead came a
>   color and a light,
> As I have seen the rosy red flushing in the
>   northern night."

The image is enhanced by Tennyson's use of color ("pallid," "rosy red") and descriptive nouns ("light," "northern night"), and in these lines we grasp something a less skilled writer might take two paragraphs to write: a woman with surging emotion unable to hide her feelings.

This portrait — its conceptual presentation — is the essence of art, and for the nonfiction writer such image-creation is essential if his or her prose seeks a level of artistry. Nonfiction writers must be aware that levels such as this are attainable if only they approach their work more creatively and less self-consciously. Image-creation is a tool of the artist's trade, and nonfiction writers can use it, too.

See, for example, *Pilgrim at Tinker Creek*, Annie Dillard's year-long self-absorbed examination of nature and the environment near her home in Virginia's Blue Ridge Mountains. Annie Dillard is a poet, first, and this is her initial nonfiction book. As might be expected, she uses poetic flair with language and conceptual development to offer singular dimension to mundane objects, effects and circumstances. Here she is describing a poisonous copperhead just a few feet away:

> "Here was this blood-filled, alert creature, this nerved rope of matter, really here instead of not here, splayed soft and solid on a rock by the slimmest of chances. It was a thickening of the air spread from a tip, a rush into being, eyeball and blood, through a pin-hole . . ."

Note the imagery: adjectives ("blood-filled," "alert," "nerved," "soft," "pinhole":), descriptive nouns ("creature," "matter," "tip," "eyeball and blood," "rent") and image-making, dramatic verbs ("splayed," "spread," "rush"). In these few words she has provided a clear picture of the snake and its ominous presence. How different it would have been if she had written:

"I came upon a poisonous copperhead, not
moving, and I was able to look him over . . ."

This latter is clearly not art, even though it may be fact, and
while the writer may have our attention (because any reference
to a poisonous snake should get our attention!), we have trouble picturing the scene. Art transcends fact, making it offer more
than the simple conclusion that something happened. Here,
Annie Dillard has made art from fact by developing images
which show the characteristics of the snake that only a sharp-
eyed observer seeing things in imagery could produce.

Most writers come to understand that putting words on
the page carries a dual effect for the reader: it isn't only what
the reader can see, it's what the reader can hear, too! What we
write can, and does, resonate in the reader's ear to the extent
that if our word–sounds clash and screech, it will affect the
reader's enjoyment of our prose. Some call this "the music of
words," and there's little doubt that as we read we take in both
the sense of the words and their sounds. Think of this well-
known Christmas nursery rhyme:

"'Twas the night before Christmas, and
All through the house, not a creature was
Stirring, not even a mouse . . ."

The sense of the words tells us that on Christmas Eve in this
house all was quiet and serene . . . and the word–sounds echo
that (note the soft word–sounds "'twas," "night," "all,"
"through," "stirring"; note, too, the gentle rhyme of "house" with
"mouse"). The "music" of these words offers lilt and sublimity.

But suppose it had been written this way:

"On Christmas Eve the house was empty,
Nothing happening, gag-quiet . . ."

Is there "music" in these words? The sense of the passage is the same, but the words convey no sweetness, no gentleness. The sounds are harsher ("empty," "happening," "gag-quiet"), and whatever word-music we can discern is probably more dissonant than smooth-blend. Its effect, therefore, is severely limited, and a nonfiction writer seeking to weave artistry into his or her prose would avoid such application.

Yet we must recognize that what we write affects what the reader hears, and this provides us with a major artistic device to beef up our nonfiction. As writers, particularly over the past couple of generations, have discovered, words and phrases which appeal primarily to the reader's *ear* can portray scenes and images just as effectively as words which are designed to be read.

Some of this comes out of the 1960s with the so-called "new journalism" which took straight fact-reporting and added a fiction-like patina in order to expand dramatic possibilities. Deep character development, extended dialogue, scene-intercutting, removal of reportorial distance and overwhelming use of first person were some of the techniques, and the results were to change the face of nonfiction forever. For the first time nonfiction writing could aspire to artistry because now it had the ability to develop storyline and related effects just as fiction did. The chains were off, and nonfiction writing blossomed.

In terms of artistry, though, an appeal to the reader's ear was paramount because this has always been one distinguishing factor between fiction (or poetry) and nonfiction; fiction could do it, nonfiction couldn't. If nonfiction could develop word music such as enhanced fiction, the line between them would narrow and weaken. Nonfiction could take its place as an art form, too.

One of the earliest developers of word-music for the reader's ear was Tom Wolfe, considered by some the father of the "new journalism." What he did was to take word-sounds, put them on the page, spell them as they sounded and expect the thought inside the word-sounds to convey his message. Here he is in the opening paragraph of an essay about Las Vegas from his 1965 book, *The Kandy-Kolored Tangerine-Flake Streamline Baby:*

> "Hernia, hernia, hernia, hernia, hernia, hernia . . .
> HERnia; hernia, HERnia, hernia . . . eight is the
> point, the point is eight . . ."

These "hernias" are repeated thirty times before he gives it up briefly . . . and then starts in again. What he's doing is mimicking the craps dealer at a major Las Vegas casino. Try and say the word quickly, over and over, running the syllables together . . . and suddenly we have a close approximation of what it's like to belly-up to a craps table as half a dozen bettors drop chips and cash on the green and white felt and the dice are bounced against the padded side.

We *hear* this scene as much as or more than we read it, and the effect can be electric: the word-sounds create an image which carries dramatic certainty. What Tom Wolfe does is to add a dimension to our concept of the written word, inviting us to understand his nonfiction by reading and hearing it. Clearly, there's artistry here because his appeal is to our senses, to our impressionistic selves, and in the way he treads the same path as artists through the ages. We *feel* what he is writing just as if it were a work of fiction or poetry such as *Confessions of Felix Krull, Confidence Man* by Thomas Mann (where, in one scene, the character speaks of his mouth watering as he describes a table laden with chocolates and smoked fish and earthy truffles) or *Sonnets From the Portugese* by Elizabeth Barrett Browning (where she explores in sense-filled words the full dimensions of her love for Robert Browning).

But there's more to what Wolfe writes because he is also setting up a rhythm, a beat that we can follow. *Hernia, hernia, hernia* . . . . Note the pulsating, repetitive sounds, their constancy, their single-mindedness and how they draw us into the scene. This rhythmic portrayal shows us musical form and in the process touches on artistry because it conceptualizes what might otherwise be uninspired fact. Do we find it in other writing forms?

How about this:

> "We're — foot — slog — slog — slog — sloggin'
>   over Africa!
> Foot — foot — foot — foot — sloggin' over
>   Africa —
> (Boots — boots — boots — boots — movin'
>   up and down again!)"

This is the poem *Boots* by Rudyard Kipling and refers to British army service around the turn of the 19th century in Africa. Note how he is appealing to our ears by the repetitive use of a single word. As we read this poem, don't we get the idea of an army marching, marching, marching . . . ? What Kipling does is to reinforce the sense of the poem by allowing us to hear his words and put ourselves in the middle of the scene.

If Kipling uses the music of words with his poetry, why

can't Tom Wolfe use it with his prose? And does it matter whether Wolfe's work is fiction or nonfiction? Isn't it artistry that counts?

Use of repetitive word-sounds is clearly an artistic device because it builds an image through an appeal to more than one sense. We conceptualize the scene, and in the process come to understand and feel more deeply and more fully.

See how scientist Oliver Sacks uses a repetitive style to give substance to a single thought — why do we "name" things, why is it important? His book, *Seeing Voices,* is an exploration of deafness, and he discovers the hearing-impaired have an obsession with naming. Why do we name, he asks?

> "It has to do, surely, with the primal power of
> words, to define, to enumerate, to allow mastery
> and manipulation, to move from the realm of
> objects and images to the world of concepts
> and names . . ."

His use of the infinitive phrase introduces thoughts and concepts in a rhythmic manner expanding our understanding of this one thought: why do we name things? Note the steady beat of the concepts: to . . . define . . . enumerate . . . allow mastery and manipulation . . . move . . . and we see each of these is significant because it balances the other ideas. This is not impressionistic writing such as Tom Wolfe offers; instead, it is "parallel repetitiveness," a technique that builds up importance through a drum beat of steady surge (like the cumulative effect of waves upon a rock). It is the buildup of concepts, steadily offered, parallel clauses or phrases, that broaden the scene and give it dimension. Even without Oliver

Sacks we might understand why hearing–impaired people label everything, but it wouldn't seem so crucial unless we lived in the same world as they do. But read over his words, the urgency of the infinitives, their solid purpose, and maybe then we can really sense the hearing-impaired's need and obsession. By using repetitive phrasing, Sacks has employed the musician's technique of reversion to the melody line, over and over, until the entire work is built around it . . . only in this case the melody line of the music becomes the infinitive phrase for the writing. This parallel repetitiveness creates a stronger image for the reader because — like the melody line — it makes the entire work stronger.

Here, then, is a different form of artistry, not so much "hearing" the words as sensing their significance for the over-all story. If a writer can conceptualize his thoughts in such a way that he adds power and substance to a human act such as "labelling" or "naming," he has created something that wasn't there before. If artistry balances on the act of creation, then Oliver Sacks has developed art. Think of it this way: one definition of art is to believe that without our exposure to the piece of art, we would never have achieved the place where the art has taken us. Our exposure to Oliver Sacks means we now have a clear understanding and empathy for the hearing-impaired and their obsession for labelling and naming.

Would we have gotten there without Sacks and his drum beat of parallel repetitiveness?

The only true answer is to be found by trying his technique and seeing where it takes us. Conceptualize first . . . then create an appropriate parallel repetitiveness (infinitives, descriptive phrases, even singular words) and see how it works. Have we created something that wasn't there before? Could it be art?

PART TWO

The Dramatic
Techniques

1.

Conflict Development

An editor was speaking about a celebrated nonfiction writer. "One day," the editor said, "the advertising manager of a successful young company mentioned that the company's president and founder was about to retire. Would the writer do a company history so the president could take it into retirement? It didn't have to be exciting, the writer was told, just something to pass around the clubroom."

The editor continued: "The advertising manager said the files were in chronological order and the story was there waiting. The writer said, 'No sir, that's not the story I'll write. What I want is the answer to two questions. Then, I'll write you something they'll pass around *outside* the clubroom' . . . ."

What the writer wanted to know was this: who was the villain in the company story and why? Every good story, the writer believed, had a villain, even something relatively tame, like a company history.

The editor added: "This writer always looked for a villain — it didn't matter what he was writing. It would be someone who stood in the way of success or satisfaction for the good guys, and once you've established that, the story almost writes itself."

Actually, it isn't as easy as this, but what the writer was saying certainly needs underscoring because there is elemental truth here. Any story rises and falls on what it says to the reader, and we know that what attracts and holds readers is the sense they are part of the unfolding story. Some refer to it as reader identification, others as dramatic impact, but the point is that as we set out our story, we have to be aware how it will affect the reader. Do we still have the reader's attention, are we confusing the reader, is the reader rooting for one of the characters? . . . all of these concerns must be in our minds as we write.

In a singular sense this is what the writer was saying: search for the villain because that, right away, will establish the viability of the story. I don't need anything else, the writer says, you give me the villain and I can take things from here.

For us, the translation is: show me a villain and I'll show you conflict. Show me conflict and I'll show you a struggle. Show me struggle, and I'll show you drama. Show me drama, and I'll show you readers paying attention. Show me readers paying attention, and I'll show you a happy writer.

The key, of course, is conflict. Without it most stories fail, and we know, even from our early writing days, that conflict and tension are inherent in any good story.

That's certainly true with fiction . . . and it's equally as true with nonfiction. If conflict is necessary for fiction to work, why shouldn't the same be true with nonfiction? Conflict is a device for developing drama, and all writers — fiction writers as well as nonfiction writers — understand that drama and dramatic impact touch and hold readers. Where fiction writers may have to create their conflict, the nonfiction writer has it in front as part of the unfolding story. Take a look at the morning newspaper, the essence of local fact-sharing. Read over the front page and note the stories — actual, *true* stories, bursting with conflict. How about the mayor at odds with a citizens' group over parking concessions; or a dispute in city council over how to divide up state reimbursements; or local student aptitude scores falling from the year before? These are conflict-laden situations, and each is nonfiction.

Novelist Janet Burroway calls conflict "the fundamental element" in fiction because in literature "only trouble is interesting." But what's true for fiction also works with nonfiction. If trouble is interesting, that means readers will pay attention, and "trouble" can appear on the fiction page or the nonfiction page. (For an example of the latter, see any true wilderness account.) What, after all, is trouble other than some situation where there is struggle? And doesn't struggle mean two opposing forces and doesn't that result in conflict and tension?

Philip Gerard in his book, *Creative Nonfiction,* leaves no doubt: "But all good nonfiction contains conflict . . . . It's no accident that the subjects which attract nonfiction writers most frequently are subjects rife with conflict . . . ." He looks to nature writing and sees wonderful examples: the material environment in steady conflict with the modern technological world. There is always conflict in nature, inherent in the forces that abide there, and Gerard sees them underpinning most of the writing. He cites Henry David Thoreau's *Walden* as a classic example. The conflict, almost from the first page, is between busy, materialistic civilization and the simple life that can be led outside that world. Thoreau writes:

"I see young men, my townsmen, whose misfortune it is to have inherited farms, houses, barns, cattle,

and farming tools; for these are more easily acquired
than gotten rid of. Better if they had been born in
the open pasture and suckled by a wolf, that they
might have seen with clearer eyes what field they
were called to labor in . . ."

It's a theme he'll follow throughout his essays, and the
continuing conflict keeps readers on their toes because he is
challenging the orthodoxy of his time: the acquisition of property, the development of material wealth. What makes it
"interesting" is his avowed determination in the face of the
large majority arrayed against him and his struggle to make a
life in this wilderness. In a real sense Thoreau, in one work,
embodies the classic conflict choices: man against nature (will
he physically survive in the wilderness?), man against man
(will he maintain his individualism in the face of beckoning,
encroaching civilization?), man against himself (will he keep
his psychological balance in the solitude of his daily life?). It
is these conflict choices that mark us as we set about developing our story. Just as they apply in fiction (think of
Hemingway's *Old Man and the Sea* where the fisherman,
Santiago, struggled with himself, with the elements and with
those who would impoverish him), they work with nonfiction,
too. Any good nonfiction writing, whether essay, narrative
account, biographical exposé, journalistic investigation, political or cultural analysis, will contain one or more of these conflict choices because that's what makes the writing "interesting" and accomplished nonfiction writers understand this.

Memoir-writing is a form of nonfiction that lends itself to
conflict-laden situations. The reason's simple: we're writing
about ourselves or about things that happened to people close
to us, and it's only human to cast ourselves in bright, positive

light most of the time. But to round out our memoir we often have to cast others in semi-darkness so that we continue to sparkle, and that means creating or developing that "villain." Then we have conflict, and in a memoir it means we've got a good guy/bad guy scenario.

And the bad guy is rarely us!
But the conflict, oh the conflict!

Sometimes a memoir will kick off the tension on the first page, and this will hold the story together for a long time. That's the way it is in Mary Karr's *The Liar's Club*, a story of growing up poor but feisty in the Texas oil fields of the early 1960s. The story begins with the author depicting a horrific scene in the middle of the night, of herself at nine years of age, in her nightgown wandering about the house while policemen scour the rooms and the local doctor asks her again and again how she's feeling. She doesn't tell us what actually happened until midway through the book, but note how the author sets up the conflict from the first line. The following are the opening sentences from the first six paragraphs in this memoir:

— "My sharpest memory is of a single instant
  surrounded by dark . . ."
— "It took three decades for that instant to unfreeze . . ."
— "I had a knee-jerk fear of the sheriff based on my
  father's tendency to get in fights . . ."
— "It was over time that the panorama became animate,
  a scene in some movie crystal ball . . ."
— "And the volume on the night began to rise . . ."
— "More door slams, the noise of boots, and some
  radio static from the cruiser on the road . . ."

By the time we've read these first six paragraphs we're totally wrapped in the story because we know there's been trouble, and we're dying to find out what it is. Why are we so interested? Because this author, even though she's but nine years old, is depicting herself in a struggle, and we're caught up in wondering what happened. Near the end of the scene the author informs us she'll be holding back the details for a later time in the book, and while that may seem unfair since she did build up our expectations so intensely, it's not a scene-killer, only an impatience-throttler.

But the point is this: nonfiction or fiction, we can begin our conflict on the first page, and it will work just fine.

One sure way to latch on to tension and conflict is to weave the story against a background of a controversial issue. The very nature of the issue will provide the necessary tension for the story. Take abortion, for example. Is there any doubt this issue is a lightning rod for controversy, that its mere presence on an agenda or in a private conversation creates severe contention? Suppose we wanted to write something about abortion's effect on the families of medical people who perform or refuse to perform abortions? By its nature this story would contain conflict because the issue, itself, is controversial. Imagine the family of an abortion clinic nurse, for example: can we assume every family member is totally supportive, can we assume none of them has ever had a confrontation inside or outside the family because of the services the nurse provides? The key for the nonfiction writer is to locate those family tension points in order to write meaningfully about what it's like to have an abortion-provider within the family.

Start with a controversial subject, and the conflict situations almost come packaged, ready to use, and here again the line between fiction and nonfiction doesn't exist. Fiction writers might craft a controversial environment such as frightfully mean psychiatric hospital or a search for illegal buried treasure, but nonfiction writers can find equally controversial environments in the real world such as unfair gamesmanship by a professional tennis player or a memoir of incest. It's not a contest to see who can offer the greatest controversy — fiction or nonfiction — but a recognition that whether the subject is medical abuse or treasure-seeking, hurtful sports activity or family abuse, the conflict within the controversial subject is clear and unambiguous. All it takes is a writer clear-eyed enough to make something of it.

One of the more comfortable ways to develop conflict with nonfiction is through the personal essay. Here, at least, we are giving our opinion, something that we feel and we wish to share with the rest of the world. Most of the time we use the first person because it is our opinion we are offering, and it can carry more force if the reader understands that. Several years ago the editor of a national magazine asked me to write a personal essay on any topic I wished, and I chose book censorship, on why people try to ban books. I knew my subject well, but I wrote in the third person, analyzing the mind-set of those who would censor. The editor returned the piece to me and said he couldn't use it. "If I wanted to know why, I'd have gone to a psychologist," he said. "I wanted your opinion, your experiences, your anger to show through. I want to know why you're mad as hell!"

That's when I realized the personal essay could be dramatic and provocative as well as informing. Think conflict, I learned, and things will fall into place. Here's what essayist Eileen Herbert Jordan says:

"*Get mad, but don't get cranky*. It is good for the
soul and good for the reader to sound off in
print about something that makes you *mad*. Take
a stand, fight for what you believe, a small issue
or a giant one . . . what you *don't* want to do is
simply to bemoan the dreary state of the world . . ."

When she speaks of growing "mad," what she's really saying is to ratchet up the controversy in what we write. To bring
in conflict, to develop opposition, and in doing this we'll spark
an interest in the reader which should hold attention until the
end. Take a look at the op-ed page in any daily newspaper,
and the chances are there will be a personal essay offering a
writer's point of view on a topic of current interest. It might
deal with a cultural matter or a political one or even a reli-
gious one, but the writer will have taken a stand, and an issue
will be joined. The key is this: find something that offends;
sharpen the conflict by pointing out who and what has been
hurt or damaged by the conduct or the event and let the world
know that a change needs to be made. In this simple formula
there is conflict, there is controversy, and it is nonfiction with
drama and certainty.

It isn't only the op-ed piece of a few hundred words that
fits the "get mad, don't get cranky" formula; we can find it in
longer works, too. Obviously, the writer can't keep a high tone
of anger on every page of a book-length work because the
reader would soon tire of the rhetoric, but judiciously applied
good anger can add substantially to literary merit and carry
the story along. Such was the case with Janet Malcolm, a *New
Yorker* writer, who looked into the lawsuit filed by convicted
murderer Jeffrey MacDonald against journalist Joe McGinnis
who had written a book, *Fatal Vision*, about MacDonald's trial

for murdering his wife and two small children. MacDonald and his defense team had invited McGinnis to witness all the preparation, planning and strategies for their case and then write his book, on the assumption that McGinnis believed MacDonald innocent of the charges. But when McGinnis's book came out, after MacDonald had been convicted, McGinnis wrote he believed MacDonald had committed the crimes. MacDonald subsequently sued McGinnis for fraud, claiming the journalist had duped the defense in order to get material for his book. At this point Janet Malcolm took a look and didn't like what she saw. She interviewed all the parties in the lawsuit, did some independent investigation and published her own book, *The Journalist and the Murderer*, which essentially skewers the journalist profession and McGinnis especially for not playing fair with interview subjects and the public generally. She didn't focus on whether MacDonald did or didn't commit the crimes, but rather on the tactics McGinnis used to extract information and cooperation from MacDonald and those around him before, during and after the trial. She was clear in her conclusion: if MacDonald had known McGinnis thought him guilty at any point during their association, McGinnis's book would never have contained the personal, close-up material it did have, and it probably would not have achieved the success it had.

Here, then, is a work of nonfiction where the writer has a definite opinion and wants to share it with the world. Malcolm's words teem with her indignation about journalism's uneven playing field where the journalist has a built-in advantage over the subject of a story and how often — as in the MacDonald-McGinnis case — advantage has been taken by the journalist. But Malcolm stays coldly analytical, showing where she felt missteps by both parties took place. At no time does she get "cranky," in the sense of bemoaning the general state of journalism. What she zeroes in on is this case, where she felt McGinnis, at times, abdicated his role as neutral journalist. It is this conflict — between McGinnis the journalist *and* book writer — that most disturbs her. She writes:

> "What gives journalism its authenticity and vitality is the tension between the subject's blind self-absorption and the journalist's skepticism. Journalists who swallow the subject's account whole and publish it are not journalists but publicists . . ."

When applied to McGinnis what she's saying is that by becoming part of the defense team, McGinnis abdicated his role as journalist, and this was especially true when he never let on to MacDonald how he felt about his guilt. For Janet Malcolm this was most disturbing, and in her account the conflicts she saw and felt in journalistic behavior were clear and unambiguous. She portrayed them well, and we the readers could follow each step along the way . . . and feel as if we were part of her story. The conflicts she portrayed formed the dramatic essence for her book, and this, more than anything else, was what held the reader.

We can't leave the general subject of conflict without a recognition that often it is the way we write something rather than what we write that can develop tension and keep the reader in lockstep. Note the difference in these two sentences:

— His car forced me off the road . . .
— I was being forced off the road by his car . . .

Which sentence has more zip, more impact? Obviously the top line, and the reason is because of the voice used. It is the *active* voice of the verb "to force" rather than its passive voice, which is what the lower line offers. The active voice occurs when the subject of the sentence (the car) does the acting ("forced"); the passive voice occurs when the subject of the sentence (the car) is acted upon ("being forced"). As the voice names suggest their effects are different: stylistically speaking, if we seek to set a mellow, laid-back mood, the passive voice would be more appropriate; for a harder-hitting, more dramatic mood, the active voice would work better. Both are certainly effective with nonfiction, but when we're developing conflict or seeking an opportunity to portray it, the active voice is more useful.

The late highly respected editor, William Sloane, had this to say:

> "The core of our language is the verb, the word
> that denotes an action, whether transitive, intransitive
> or reflexive. The vigor and precision of a nonfiction
> passage can almost be gauged by the proportion of
> verbal-force words it contains. Passive verb forms
> often signal authorial hedging or limpness of
> thinking . . ."

His designation of "verbal-force" words is another way of saying that active-voice verbs are a better choice for nonfiction. Regardless of whether we agree or not the point he makes is valuable because it shows that even to the verb-form used we must be aware of how it impacts the level of conflict and drama with our nonfiction.

If we're writing history:

Lincoln ordered General Meade to march . . .

not

General Meade was ordered by Lincoln to march . . .

If we're writing a memoir:

My father walked the fence line each day . . .

not

The fence line was walked by my father each day . . .

If we're doing an essay:

The wilderness trail showed no sign of animal traffic . . .

not

No animal traffic was showing on the wilderness trail . . .

The same principles apply to any form of nonfiction including straight journalism, biography, science-writing, sports-writing and so forth. Of course, there will be occasions when we don't want or need to beef up the conflict, and then our verb-form may not be so crucial. But the important thing to remember is this:

Conflict is like a good, reliable friend: it's there when we want to use it, and if we treat it right, it can make our nonfiction dramatic, memorable and reader-friendly.

Can a writer ask for more than that?

2.

Provide Anecdotes!

When I greet new writing students, I have a well-honed litany:

You've chosen a course that will test your imagination and your patience, and if you find things come easily for you, then I'm not doing my job. Writing is hard work, yet I hope you come away with a heightened sense of what it means to entrance others with words. From our earliest days, we learned to say, "Tell me a story," and we readied ourselves for an imaginative journey that took us away from the here and now, and transported us to somewhere different . . .

Stories, I emphasize, are all around us, and it is the writer's skill — and the writer's art — to recognize them and make them readable . . . and enjoyable! Stories are the cauldron where drama bubbles; stories offer the chance to think and dream and experience as if we're someone else or somewhere else.

Stories, in essence, are the foundation for literary art, and we need to understand that stories contain the seeds that turn an unremarkable event into something meaningful, and thus become an art form.

Think story, story, story! I tell the students.

Because *that's* what we're conditioned to expect — "tell me a story" . . . we've heard it, we've said it, we've enjoyed it. As writers we should be able to give it special articulation. We know, too, that stories sometimes come wrapped in other, larger stories.

These we call anecdotes. They are vignettes of some larger happening that bears on the overall tale. Anecdotes come without the complications a full story can have. In an analogy to the power of sight, anecdotes are glimpses while the broader story is a *stare* . . .

Like this:

I find the pealing ring of a cell phone in a quiet place a gross intrusion. Is this where the Age of Inconsideration has reached? I overheard a young woman in the library announce one day to a caller: "I can talk for hours, it's so nice and quiet around here." Did she wonder about disturbing me or the others? That's what gets me . . .

And this:

One day while I was reading in the library, I heard a cell phone ring nearby. A young woman answered it and broke out laughing. "No problem," she said, "I have the details right here." She rummaged through her bag and came out with a sheaf of papers. "Let me read this to you," she said, "it's not that long." A pause and then a giggle. "No, silly, that's for later . . . "

Is there a difference between these? They both are on the same subject: the narrator witnesses and hears the phone conversation each time, the scenes take place in the library. BUT . . .

In the first selection, the change in story lasts only four lines, beginning "I overheard . . . ", and when the narrator says "That's what gets me" the story reference is over. We know the narrator is about to discuss his personal reaction to these intrusions, and in doing this he has moved away from the story reference to the young woman.

In the second selection, however, the story reference runs for the entire length of the selection, and it reads as if the storyline will continue. Certainly, when the young woman giggles and throws out a line about something being "for later," the writer had better not drop us here. We, the readers, want to know *what's* for later and *why* is it for later? So the writer needs to plunge on and develop a more substantial story.

In the first instance we have an anecdote, even if it's just four lines long. It's a *glimpse*, not a *stare*, and it's all we'll need to see and feel drama in the personal essay about the Age of Inconsideration. Contrast the second selection where conflict between narrator and young woman seems to be building, and we know there needs to be much more story room for it to play out. In fact, the conflict might, in and of itself, *be* the story, and so the idea of anecdote is superfluous.

When we search for dramatic technique, however, one of the most reliable forms is the use of an anecdote. "Tell me a story . . . " is its operative effect, but in writer-talk it means we're dramatizing and developing artistic flair. Sally-Jo Bowman said it plainly in a writer's magazine article a few years ago: "Use anecdotes, and you are guaranteed to show rather than tell."

Show instead of tell! Simple words, simple comments — most of us know exactly what she means. Showing provides a mental image, it allows for dramatic effect and draws the reader into the story. Telling means lecturing, *not* providing an image, *not* emphasizing dramatic effect.

This is showing:

John wished he could stop the pounding behind his eyes, the throbbing that sent flashes of pain all the way to the back of his throat . . .

This is telling:

John was in bad pain. His head hurt and he didn't know how to stop it . . .

In the first case we have a mental image, John in deep pain, feeling it, suffering, and we suffer along with him. In the second case we know John's in pain, but where's the mental image? There's nothing to tie us to John, and so we can't identify with him.

It's the same with an anecdote. As Bowman says, the anecdote can be used to show rather than tell, and the reason is that it provides drama through the medium of storytelling. It's a classic example, in fact: *Tell me a story* . . .

The basic thing to realize is that anecdotes don't have to be long or involved. The first selection about the young woman in the library and the cell phone is all that's needed. In four lines we've told a story, and the reader's attention is fixed. *Tell me a story* is what it took.

See how Saul Bellow does it with his essay, "It All Adds

Up," about television anchor men as modern day pundit-successors to Walter Lippman and whether they know enough to justify their high place in the national consciousness. He accomplishes the anecdote in a few short sentences;

> "On a talk show not long ago, a prominent African-American declared that the Roosevelt administration had closely supported Hitler until the Pearl Harbor attack. The journalists on his panel made no objection to this. Had none of them heard of Lend-Lease?"

He offers a few more rhetorical questions to establish the wrong-headedness of the comment, and then he concludes:

> "Can these high-finish, well-tailored and well-hairstyled interviewers know so little about history?"

For Saul Bellow, the answer is probably in the affirmative, and he is rightly struck by the nonsensical credibility afforded these single-dimension characters. But note how less effective it would have been if he had said:

> I don't think television anchor people are very bright. They don't know history, and they don't understand global politics . . .

Clearly, this kind of writing would have brought the ho-hums because the drama wasn't there. How different it is when the writer starts: "One day . . . " and then launches into an anecdote! We can *see* the scene Bellow develops, we can picture it:

Fade In . . . a television studio, four well-dressed men
sitting at a shiny table, serious expressions
on their faces One of the men, an African-
American, is leaning forward and speaking:

Albert Anchorman
No doubt in my mind FDR and his people
were in Hitler's corner until Pearl Harbor.
They let France fall, didn't they? And what
about all those air raids over Britain? No
help from Washington either . . .

Camera . . . slowly pans expressions of other panelists:
one nods, another smiles briefly, a third purses his lips . . .

This is the scene Saul Bellow creates with his anecdote,
and the mental image sticks. Nothing like this could happen
if there were no drama to develop. The anecdote, short though
it might have been, tells a story, and the reader is in step.

It should be obvious that anecdotes function as easily in
nonfiction as they do with fiction. The only major difference,
of course, is that with nonfiction the anecdote itself must be
truthful, must actually have happened. But for many nonfiction writers good research will turn up enough information so
an anecdote can be developed and ultimately used. Still, there
appears to be a bit of room for the nonfiction writer to do a little "fictionalizing" even in this instance. Some years ago
Franklynn Peterson and Judi Kesselman Turkel wrote *The
Author's Handbook*, and they offer a guide to what the nonfiction writer may do:

" . . . many nonfiction writers fictionalize names, places,

and other story elements to protect their sources or
to heighten the points they are trying to make. So
even in this regard, there's often little difference
between an anecdote and a scene in fiction . . . ."

What they are saying is that an anecdote is a story in the
sense that it has earmarks of what it takes to create a fiction
scene: there is drama, characterization, dialogue perhaps,
some mood or atmosphere development . . . the list could go
on. The authors make it plain that given the opportunity to do
so nonfiction writers should avail themselves of fiction-writing
approaches as they go about developing their story.
"Effectively used the anecdote *takes the place* of exposition,
the laying out of your facts . . . " and the anecdote does this
by spinning a yarn that whets reader interest.

But what of the limitations of the nonfiction model? After
all, we're constrained by the facts, we can't simply invent a
story, make it an anecdote and insert it in our tale of something that actually happened. Sure, the argument goes, we
can use certain fiction-writing devices to give oomph to our
story, but we can only take that so far . . . once we cross into
the realm of make-believe where fiction writers live and
breathe, we'd better make sure the reader knows about it.
Otherwise we're going to have explaining to do because once
we get the reader thinking that our story is a true recounting
of an event that actually happened, they'll cry foul! when we
suddenly change the rules.

And they have every right to be upset. Two questions will
gnaw at them:

— if it's fiction now, how much can I believe about
the earlier part?

— is this writer playing games with me?

Either way, the writer's in trouble with these readers because they haven't been let in on things from the beginning. Readers feeling that way respond in the most basic manner: they stop reading the writer's work!

But according to Peterson and Turkel we don't have to bend the anecdote into a fictional pretzel in order to achieve and push the notion of drama. The anecdote can, and should, remain nonfiction because the surrounding story is also non-fiction. But the appropriate result — dramatic effect — can still be gained by the very nature of what the anecdote accomplishes. "The ring of truth in an anecdote," they say, "is achieved by seeing all the vivid details and making the reader see them too."

Isn't this exactly what a fiction writer does? Details are the pieces that make up the picture, and they become impressive when they are vividly portrayed. For example, in the fiction writer's world, an untrained stallion can be described: "muscle-rippled flanks that set off a waving, silvery mane which sparkled with the lather of his determination . . . ." The details, when they are vivid enough, paint the picture, and any accomplished fiction writer understands this.

But it's also true with nonfiction. Vivid details can paint a fine picture here, as well. Look no further than Sebastian Junger's *The Perfect Storm* where high sea adventure, danger and ultimate death are portrayed. In the middle of a huge storm, a small fishing boat is struck by a massive wave:

"It blows out a portside window with the sound of a shotgun going off. Water inundates the bridge and barrels down the hallway . . . "

The nonfiction details here are what paint the picture and give it drama. Windows blown out, water barrelling — these are what stick in the reader's mind and provide the image the author is striving to develop.

Apply this to an anecdote, and the same thing happens. The "ring of truth" comes through because of the vivid details, and the nonfiction writer need not over-develop, or over-emphasize, the fact that the story actually happened.

See how details help to dramatize an anecdote in Norman Cousins's book, *Anatomy of an Illness As Perceived By The Patient*. The author, in the course of writing about the history and uses of "placebos," offers an anecdote of a visit with physician and Nobel Laureate, Albert Schweitzer, in Gabon, West Africa. They have gone to observe a witch doctor:

> "With some patients the witch doctor merely put herbs
> in a brown paper bag and instructed the ill person in their
> use. With other patients, he gave no herbs but filled
> the air with incantations. A third category of patients he
> merely spoke to in a subdued voice and pointed to
> Dr. Schweitzer."

Cousins tell us that the first group received an herbal medication, the second group received an African type of psychotherapy and the third group needed surgery and were referred to Dr. Schweitzer who remarked, not without humor, "Some of my steadiest customers are referred to me by witch doctors . . . ."

Note the vividness of the details here, and the fact that the anecdote about the witch doctor doesn't take up much space. Cousins could have described the witch doctor without mentioning the brown bag containing the herbs, or the incantations (sounds which most of us can imagine) or even the reference to Dr. Schweitzer. He could have written:

> We spent a couple hours watching a witch doctor deal
> with patients. Some he spoke to, others he gave herbs
> and still others he referred to Dr. Schweitzer.

Nothing particularly dramatic here, and the anecdote
won't carry the impact that Cousins's actual text does. The
anecdote does contain that "ring of truth," if for no other reason than that Dr. Schweitzer is in the scene, and that might be
enough to provide dramatic effect. But how much more interesting it becomes when we get details about how the witch
doctor worked and what his relationship was with Dr.
Schweitzer!

That's drama and that's what holds readers.

In the flashback there are myriad ways to introduce an
anecdote, and in most cases the same words or phrases will
suffice for both. Time, for example, is always a reliable first
step: *A few years ago . . . . I remember when Mother . . . That
time we were both in school . . .* Each of these would do well
whether it's flashback or anecdote or a bit of both. But there
are differences, and we shouldn't ignore them. Simply put, all
flashbacks are anecdotes in the sense that a flashback is a
separate scene and provides some kind of story.

But the obverse — all anecdotes are flashbacks — isn't
true. Some anecdotes are not flashbacks, they don't force us
to go back in time, and they don't even have to move the story
forward. And this is equally as true with nonfiction as with fiction. For example, suppose a character is face-to-face with a
major decision, and he wants to develop a scenario to see how
his choice might fare. It could go like this (and remember this
is nonfiction):

"You know what I should do?" John said to me as he ground his cigarette on the pavement. "What I *really* should do?"

I must have shrugged because he gave me a strange look and lowered his voice. "Catch this . . . I walk in there, don't even knock . . . Boom! right in the conference room, don't take my eye off him, put the good smile on, hand in the air like the jerk's my best friend, you know? 'Hey Dal,' I say, 'need to talk, good buddy, I feel a raise comin' on, how about that?'"

There's no time factor in this, yet we have an anecdote, even if it's merely the figment of a character's imagination. It doesn't qualify as a flashback yet it provides some drama and perspective and offers a succinct little story. The point is this: anecdotes don't always have to occur in the past, they might be appropriate even in the present, and they represent a skillful device for adding drama and excitement to the story. Remember what Sally-Jo Bowman said: anecdotes make it possible to "show" rather than "tell," and there are no time-of-occurence limits on their use.

On the other hand, flashbacks can go on for pages, even for chapters, while anecdotes are more limited. In most cases anecdotes are over and done with rather quickly; they don't linger or hang around. There's a very good reason for this: if an anecdote stretches on for pages, it ceases to remain an anecdote after a while; it becomes the main story because so much of what is going on resides in the tale now being told. For writers it means we have to understand from the beginning which will be our main story and which will remain anecdotes. And we have to sculpt our anecdotes so they remain what they are and don't intrude on or usurp portions of the main story. Anecdotes should *highlight* the main story, not overwhelm it.

Take a look at the work of Jessica Mitford and her renowned book, *The American Way of Death,* written almost forty years ago. It was published about the same time as the early work of the "new journalists" such as Tom Wolfe and Hunter Thompson began to develop, but it was much more a traditional piece of nonfiction — that is, she didn't indulge in a bevy of fictional devices to move her story along. This was an extraordinary piece of investigative journalism except for one crucial item: she injected herself into the story, and in this manner she did mirror the new journalists who made a practice of placing themselves at the heart of any story they were writing and presenting their own, first-person point of view. Mitford does this, too, though she's careful to let many of her observations speak for themselves and not carry a particular characterization.

Yet the drama inherent in her subject — how much it costs to die in America — is palpable and doesn't need much fictional-device fixing. She does offer anecdotes, however, and in this way the existing drama is heightened. Here she is, for example, relating a phone call she made to a leading San Francisco undertaker concerning the impending demise of a (fictional) elderly aunt. The family, she told him, wanted something simple, just cremation, no service at all. They would prefer not to buy a coffin:

> "The undertaker's voice at the other end was now alert, although smooth. He told me, calmly and authoritatively, that it would be 'illegal' for him to enter into such an arrangement. 'You mean, it would be against the law?' I asked. Yes indeed . . . I tried two more funeral establish-

ments and was told substantially the same thing: cremation of an uncoffined body is prohibited by California law."

Yet when she checked with the Board of Health she was told there was no law which prohibited cremation of an uncoffined body. Clearly, this is a dramatic moment in her story: she has caught the California funeral establishment in some sort of conspiratorial untruth, but note how she handles it. The anecdote is short, even if the point is weighty. She doesn't belabor extracting the information, merely sets out what she was told and what she was able to find that contradicted it. The drama inherent in this situation needs no revving up, and she recognizes it. Conflict, misinformation and possible exploitation of humans at a vulnerable moment make for a riveting storyline, and when it's nonfiction, it simply supports the old idea about fact being more interesting than . . .

Oh well . . . just keep the anecdotes short, and they'll work magic.

3.

Develop That Character!

How's this for an opening?

At the end of page one the author describes Bobby Shatford, lying asleep under the sheet.

At the top of page two the author goes on:

"He's got one black eye. There are beer cans and food wrappers scattered around the room and a duffel bag on the floor with T-shirts and flannel shirts and blue jeans spilling out. Lying asleep next to him is his girlfriend, Christina Cotter . . ."

Maybe we can zero in by saying what it's *not*! It's not a high-priced hotel room, it's not — probably not — Bobby Shatford's home, it's not a morning without physical discomfort looming . . .

The scene is from the opening pages of Sebastian Junger's *The Perfect Storm,* the story of deep-sea fishermen out of Gloucester, Massachusetts, and their fishing boats, their families and their lives. Bobby Shatford is a fisherman, signing on for extended voyages in fishing boats that work thousands of miles off shore, and this story will depict him and the others and the harrowing work they do and did.

The author's task was simple enough: tell the story through the eyes of the people who lived it, give the reader an opportunity to jump into the skin of someone like Bobby Shatford and see what it's *really* like facing down fifty-foot waves in a boat barely twice that length, buffeted across wave tops by seventy–mile–an–hour winds, crawling through dense fog in an ocean with no seeming end.

What Sebastian Junger did was to develop his story by setting up his characterizations, by not interposing himself between his characters and the continuing story. He could have written a steady, chronological narrative where he "tells" us what is going on, instead of "showing" us what happens. Take the selection above, and see how that would read if we wrote it differently:

> "Bobby Shatford was asleep in bed with the
> sheet over him. He'd been in a fight the night
> before, and he'd gone to bed drunk after eating
> a couple of take-out hamburgers. His girlfriend
> was asleep next to him . . ."

We get the same details, but note how differently they are portrayed. In the first selection we read he's got a black eye and there are beer cans and food wrappers around. In the latter selection we find out he had a fight, went to bed drunk and ate some take-out in his room.

But what does that tell us about his character? In our mind's eye do we know what he looks like, what he sounds like, what he thinks?

How about the first selection? At least here we get an idea of what he looks like — the black eye, of course. And we can also imagine the room in disarray, sour body smells, lingering yeasty odor of stale beer and old food . . .

In short, we know more about Bobby Shatford because our imaginations spur us on to develop a mental image. Perhaps the image isn't pretty, perhaps it's unfair, but at least the author has done his part by offering us a scene to get involved with. He has made it possible for us to jump into the story.

And this, of course, is precisely what we seek to accomplish with characterization, whether it's fiction or nonfiction. The important thing is to remember that a story tends to rise and fall on the portrayal of the characters, and character portrayal is simply an extension of drama and dramatic effect. Characters need to come alive on the page, and we do this by fleshing them out and allowing readers to blink, think and link . . . *I understand that person . . . I've met him/her before . . . I really like that character . . .*

But how do we do this, how do we flesh out the characters? Novelist Janet Burroway offers one approach for fiction writers:

> "A character can be directly revealed to us
> through *appearance, speech, action and thought . . ."*

and she goes on to suggest that if we put one of these methods at odds with any of the others, "then dramatic tension will be produced." But it can also work with nonfiction. The only difference is that nonfiction characters must actually exist. Take appearance and action. Suppose we describe a character as short and round and pudgy, cuddly-like and soft. How

52

active might we expect this character to be?

Probably sedate and sedentary, so not active at all.

Now apply Burroway's suggestion — put the appearance at odds with succeeding action . . . make our pudgy character a dynamo of activity, never still, never sedate.

Perhaps even make him violent, someone who's appearance belies his nature. Is there drama here?

Or put it a different way — are we getting what we expect here? The answer would seem to be a resounding NO!, and thus the unexpected result creates tension which, in turn, creates dramatic effect. A pudgy, cuddly man with a violent temper who likes to hurt people . . . isn't this characterization that intrigues and keeps our attention?

Try another combination — speech and thought, for example. Suppose we talk one way but think another, and they are at odds! A smiling face . . . and murderous intent . . . or patriotic comments . . . and subversive thoughts . . . or cooing words . . . and cold thoughts . . . The point is that by setting these characteristics in conflict, we get a deeper insight into the character, and the conflict, itself, offers us a dramatic opportunity.

Can we apply this to nonfiction? Take a look at Richard Rovere's study of General Douglas MacArthur and his public and private persona in "The Wicked Conspiracy Against General MacArthur." A spellbinding speaker who appealed to chivalric honor and the moral high road in public, MacArthur had an entirely different set of values in private. Rovere calls him a "true believer in himself," egocentric, messianic. "Like others of his breed," Rovere writes, "[MacArthur] finds it necessary to ascribe his disappointments, which have been numerous, to base intrigue. In his melancholy and wayward universe, there is no purely personal guilt . . . ." For the private MacArthur the fault, the blame resided elsewhere, certainly not with his plans or his decisions or his activities. For the public MacArthur the appeal went above blame, to universal values of honor and grace and high moral purpose. In his 1956 speech to a joint session of the U.S. Congress, following his abrupt dismissal by President Harry S Truman from command of U.S. forces in the Far East, he concluded with "Old soldiers never die, they just fade away." People like him, he was saying, remain true to the cause even if their services are no longer required. I have my soldierly mission, and that will not dissolve, I will remain a presence in the service of my country for a long, long time . . .

The private MacArthur and the public MacArthur, warring on the battlefield of speech and thought: Am I what I say I am or what I think I am? It provides a delicious opportunity to probe the character of the man and provide both sides of his personality. It is the essence of drama because it offers an exciting scenario where things will happen, sometimes unexpectedly, because we're never sure which aspect of MacArthur's personality will dominate at any given moment. The very complexity of the man makes him "interesting," and to a reader an interesting character is what keeps attention riveted.

Speech and thought, appearance and action — mix and match these at will with a nonfiction character because dramatic tension is there for the taking, and all that's needed is a storyline to work against.

The truest, and by far the most all-inclusive, character depiction is usually found in biography or autobiography. I use "true" in the sense of factually developed, not as a synonym for pure actuality. We've come to realize, especially with autobiography, that most writers tend to leave out that which is embarrassing or demeaning or even illegal. We recognize at best that this type of nonfiction writing is simply one writer's take on what happened, and while factually based may not be the "whole story." Yet what drives the story is the nature of the individual portrayed, and even if the storyline remains incomplete, we're bound to learn more than we knew about the character. Patricia Bosworth says the biographer (and by implication the autobiographer) should display talents of an historian, psychiatrist and novelist when going about their tale, and yet even that will provide only a measure of completeness. "If one is lucky," she says, "one comes away with the essence of a character, a version of a life. But there is always more than one version."

Any well-known public figure can attest to that. Biographies abound on ex-Presidents, ex-sports heroes, ex-show business personalities or well-known literary figures (take a look at the list of biographies on the life of Ernest Hemingway, for example, each one claiming authenticity about the niche in his life they portray). Yet the writer, for all his or her research and study and character development, can only present a version of that life. And it really can't be any other way because the writer, throughout the work, has made value judgments about what is or is not germane, what is or is not interesting, what is or is not supportable. In essence the biographer must apply those skills Patricia Bosworth mentions: historian, psychiatrist and novelist even as the storyline unfolds. The character comes to life because dramatic skills are employed.

The recent work by Edmund Morris, *Dutch,* on the life of Ronald Reagan, is a classic example. While most acknowledge it as biography, the author calls it a "memoir," claiming it's "a study in the phenomenon of memory." Yet it follows

Reagan from his earliest days right into the White House and
beyond. If biography is a "version" of a life, then this clearly
qualifies because Morris is doing exactly that — providing *his*
version of Ronald Reagan's life. And the way he does it is by
inventing a narrator — himself — and injecting this fictional
character into the book in order to add life and zest to the
story. His fictional character observes Reagan at various peri-
ods of the ex-President's life and portrays him in ways the
orthodox biography might not have been able to show. Here's
the way Morris put it in a television interview:

> "It's a story of Ronald Reagan told by myself
> but in an intensely nostalgic and memoiristic
> form and woven into it is the fabric of his own
> memories of himself and his life . . ."

Does this sound like the sort of writer we used to think
wrote nonfiction? "Intensely nostalgic" . . . "memoiristic *form*"
. . . "woven into it" . . . "fabric" . . . ? This sounds like a fiction
writer who has started with some facts and built a dramatic tale
out of his own imagination and creativity. In short, it is the biographer who has sprinkled a bit of the novelist and the historian
and the psychiatrist into his portrayal of the ex-President.

There has, of course, been a great deal of criticism of
Edmund Morris for using this technique with a literary form
that traditionally has been so fact-based. But it was precisely
because of the formal "rules" concerning biographical writing
that Morris did what he did. In the same television interview
he says he began by writing a standard political biography
about Reagan. But within two years he found it "dying on the
page." He goes on:

"He resisted orthodox analysis because Reagan
is a performer. He was a performer as a boy. He
was a performer as an old man, and a performer
is not comprehensible unless he is witnessed,
unless there's a spectator there, unless there's
an audience. I became his biographical audience . . ."

Out of the maelstrom of his concern Edmund Morris found a way to portray Reagan dramatically and with purpose. He may have turned the history/biography establishment on its head, but he also enlivened his story and provided *his* version of Ronald Reagan's character. The first time the fictional Morris character comes upon Reagan in 1926, the author has his character say:

"His face irked me. It had an adolescent
coarseness and an air of studied jollity as
as if he knew he was being watched . . ."

Later on, the fictional Morris runs into Reagan at a Dixon, Illinois, public swimming facility, and the author writes:

"Watching him — indeed, trying to imitate
him — helped me understand at least partly
the massive privacy of his personality . . ."

Traditionally, no biographer would inject himself or herself into the storyline like this, but then, too, character insights such as these would probably not be present (or at least not be so pronounced) in the traditional biography. Clearly, opinions will differ about the appropriateness of using this type of device and continuing to label the work a biography, or even a memoir, but what it shows, beyond all else, is that character can be dramatically portrayed in a work of nonfiction. And if the drama is there, then the work will find readers.

Edmund Morris is certainly not the first to toy with the conventions of biographic fact-setting, though he may have taken matters a bit further than most. But if we look at the work of Irving Stone who has written a host of books he labels "biographical novels," we see a kindred spirit.

And Stone has been doing this for decades. For example, he's written *The Origin,* about the life of Charles Darwin, and *The Greek Treasure* about the joint lives of Henry and Sophia Schliemann, the discoverers of the ancient city-state of Troy. He uses various fiction-writing devices to develop his stories, including dialogue and other drama-producing ideas that appear elsewhere in this book, yet he insists his works are nonfiction. If he didn't believe this, why would he append the prefix "biographical" to the enduring definition of his work? The storyline is factual, the characters existed, and beyond that he's willing to concede he may take some dramatic license. Hence the "novel" side of his self-created category: "biographical novel."

But it is the way he approaches characterization that's instructive for us. Since he writes biography, character and characterization are all-important, and his methods are as adaptable to nonfiction as they are to fiction. He writes:

> "In order to determine whether [my material]
> will make a biographical novel, I first have to
> determine whether or not I can understand this
> person, grasp him, whether I can realize his
> values, whether I can live through his adventures,
> his experiences, his failures, weaknesses, his

faults, his errors, his collapses, as well as
his successes, his ecstasies, accomplishments,
realizations . . ."

What he's really saying is that proper characterization requires the writer to jump into the skin of the character, to understand him or her to such an extent there is almost an alter-ego effect. Suppose we're doing a story about a character facing an emergency, and we must describe how that character will react. One way to do it would be to describe the character as some third party might see him:

He began to sweat as the awesome noise
swelled, and he held his hands over his
ears and searched the raucous crowd for some
glimpse of her, his face contorted in a mask of worry . . .

Now let's try it by getting inside the character and looking *out*:

He felt the cold sweat of panic when he couldn't
find her in the raucous crowd. The noise
deafened him, brought him stabs of terror,
made him beg silently, *I haven't lost her, no
I haven't . . . haven't! . . .*

The difference is one of dramatic effect, and as long as the nonfiction writer can base these internal feelings, thoughts and reactions on personal testimony of the character, they would seem to satisfy the conventions of biography, insofar as Irving Stone is concerned. What the writer would be doing is living "through [the character's] experiences . . . weaknesses . . . faults . . ."

And doesn't this make for a more interesting story?

John Hersey in his *Hiroshima* uses this technique with some of his character depictions in the aftermath of the August 6, 1945, atomic bomb explosion. Here he is with Father Wilhelm Kliensorge of the Society of Jesus on the morning of the explosion, who Hersey tells us is:

> " . . . in rather frail condition. The Japanese
> wartime diet had not sustained him, and
> he felt the strain of being a foreigner in an
> increasingly xenophobic Japan; even a
> German, since the defeat of the Fatherland
> was unpopular. Father Kliensorge had, at
> thirty-eight, the look of a boy growing too
> fast . . . . He walked clumsily, leaning forward
> a little. He was tired all the time . . ."

Hersey is giving us both approaches here, physical description from the outside and feelings and attitudes from the inside. Note how he puts it with Father Kliensorge looking *out*: the priest "felt the strain of being a foreigner . . . ," the priest "was tired all the time . . . ." In Irving Stone's words this character was showing "his . . . weaknesses . . . his collapses . . . ." We get inside the character and we come to understand, perhaps more deeply and more movingly, than we could have if we had stayed on the outside.

Note, too, that Hersey is giving us added material so the picture of Father Kliensorge becomes even fuller. The priest's *outward* physical characteristics, what he might look like to a spectator or an objective third party, is also provided. Hersey describes him with the look of "a boy growing too fast . . ." and what do we take away from that? Perhaps a bit gangly, unevenly proportioned where one part of his body hasn't quite caught up with the other parts: for example, wouldn't this be appropriate:

> His feet seemed too large for the rest of
> him, except for his hands, which somehow
> offered a kind of grotesque balance . . .

Hersey goes on: the priest " . . . walked clumsily, leaning forward a little . . . ." Here again there are physical characteristics which can be observed objectively from a distance; they add to our picture and provide a more thorough depiction.

But do they rev up the drama? The answer lies in the nature of the subject being written about — the scene of the most horrendous explosive device ever set off by man up to that time. The reader wants to *know* what people in the explosion zone looked like, felt like, even talked like. What was it *really* like, the reader wants to know, and so the greater the amount of detail provided by the writer — even to physical descriptions — the more the reader wants to absorb.

Hence, the dramatic effect is the image in the reader's mind left by the writer: a scene of devastation where one character can look like "a boy growing too fast . . . "and walk "clumsily, leaning forward a little . . ."

Yet, in most cases physical description will provide more than enough for the reader's image of who the writer is portraying. There's always danger in trying to get "inside" a character with nonfiction because truth and reality may be elusive and incomplete. What a writer "thinks" a character felt or didn't feel can only be as accurate as the source the writer uses for the information. An attempt to "fictionalize" in the interest of adding drama can only lead the writer into trouble.

Such, however, is not the case with objective physical description. We know what we're seeing, for example, when a character is described as "square-jawed" or "ruddy-complected" or "coat-rack thin." Dramatic effect comes when the character's physical appearance changes as a result of events, when, for example, a character's laid-back disposition suddenly grows agitated or a character's loud voice suddenly becomes soft . . .

The changes are dramatic, and each of us can picture what's happening.

See how John Berendt does it in his *Midnight In the Garden of Good and Evil,* which he labels as a work of nonfiction and the characters as "real," even though he admits to taking "storytelling liberties." His intention, however, "has been to remain truthful to the characters," and, in fact, he opens his book with character description. Note the dramatic nuances he uses as he describes the character, Jim Williams:

> "He was tall, about fifty, with darkly handsome,
> almost sinister features: a neatly trimmed mustache,
> hair turning silver at the temples, and eyes so
> black they were like the tinted windows of a
> sleek limousine — he could see out, but you
> couldn't see in . . ."

As the book progresses the shady, jaded portions of Williams's life become detailed, and we come to see him as a complicated, sexually-troubled man with an aura of elegance and sophistication. But his shady, jaded side give the book dramatic impact (because that's where the conflict and tension reside), and note how the author clues us in. Williams has:

— almost sinister features
— black-colored eyes
— eye color like sleek limousine tinted windows
— he could see out, you couldn't see in

All of these are objective physical characteristics; anyone of us could look at him and pick out the same things or have the same reaction. But note these are unsettling descriptions; each implies threat, danger, unholy purpose. And the result is a rise in dramatic impact. Berendt, in the opening lines of his book, has made his lead character controversial, and this has made his nonfiction tale something any reader would find difficult to put down because the drama is there from the beginning.

4.

Let's Do Dialogue!

⟨≈≈⟩

Two police cars speed along the highway, bound for the local jail. In each vehicle is a suspected murderer, captured only a few hours before. Dick, one of the suspects, has confessed, and the police are telling that to Perry, the other suspect, hoping it will induce him to confess, too. But Perry doesn't budge . . . until one of the officers mentions Perry had beaten a black man to death years before. Perry fixes on a deserted piece of highway and says to the police:

"I thought it was a stunt. I didn't believe you.
That Dick let fly. The tough boy! Oh, a real
brass boy. Wouldn't harm the fleas on a dog.
Just ran over the dog."

Perry spits, then says:

"I never killed any nigger. But *he* thought so. I
always knew if we ever got caught, if Dick
really ever really let fly, dropped his guts all

over the goddam floor — I knew he'd tell about
the nigger . . . "

This is a scene from Truman Capote's *In Cold Blood,* which
portrays the vicious killing of a farm family in Kansas and the
subsequent capture, trial and execution of the murderers.
Throughout the book he re-creates dialogue as if he had been
present during some of the most dramatic moments, when in
fact he couldn't have been present because the events
occurred months and years before the idea of doing the book
had come to him. His book appeared in 1965, and it was in
the vanguard of so-called "new journalism" where nonfiction
writers stepped beyond reciting facts and gave us feelings,
thoughts and extended dialogue. The key was how Capote
characterized his book; he called it a "nonfiction novel," and
this freed him to have a foot in both fiction and nonfiction
camps. In effect, he could enjoy the tastiest fruits from either,
and the result was writing certainly more dramatic than the
usual old journalism but also less accurate and certain. It
sparked a debate that rings to this day, and while this is not
the forum to examine it in detail, every writer of nonfiction
should be aware dramatizing nonfiction *too much* (that is,
without regard to the conventions of truth telling and fairness
to the reader) will bring decided and deserved criticism.

It is with dialogue that the issue is seriously joined
because the dramatic potential is so great. Dialogue is a
drama-inducing device, and its use with nonfiction can provide realism and reader involvement in ways narrative struggles to duplicate. But nonfiction writing is *not* fiction writing,
and when made-up dialogue is attached to a factual situation
the entire issue of veracity comes into question.

Take a look at the passage from Truman Capote's book.

His character is in a police car, speeding down the highway, surrounded by law men, and it's pretty clear Capote wasn't on the scene — then. But he writes the dialogue — he puts words in Perry's mouth — as if he's listening to every syllable, and the question for us, the readers, is: has Perry actually said those words or is Capote using dramatic license to convey the gist of what was said?

It's clear the dialogue propels the story and gives it more meat, and as writers we recognize the skills involved. He could have written:

Perry figured Dick had told the police about the
black man-beating story, and he had to laugh.
He'd made it up and Dick had fallen for it!

Doesn't the dialogue add richness to the account, give it a more personal flavor? Capote knew this, of course, and that's why he chose to dramatize the scene in the way he did. But he also left himself an out in case criticism about his extensive use of dialogue grew too fierce. By calling it a "nonfiction novel" he let the reader in on his intentions at the very beginning — that he would employ fiction-writing technique with this true story — and he felt, therefore, that he wasn't bound by strict, journalistic, facts-only writing.

What Capote accomplished in 1965 with dialogue has been adopted by scores of writers since then, and nonfiction writing has become livelier and more interesting as a result. Extended dialogue use now appears regularly in nonfiction, and so long as the writer makes clear at the beginning what is or was faithfully recorded (and what is or was not), the story can go on without a jaundiced jury ready to criticize.

There are poles of separation, however, between the way

different nonfiction writers approach dialogue use. Dan Kurzman, author of *Blood and Water,* the story about the destruction of the Nazi heavy water plant during World War II, published his book in 1997. In his preface, Kurzman writes:

> "All quotations, thoughts, and feelings presented here appear precisely as these individuals expressed them to me, or as they have recorded them in their diaries, memoirs, letters or war records. *Let me stress that nothing in this book is fictionalized . . .* (italics supplied)."

Kurzman is pretty clear about the scope of dramatic license here — there isn't much, and he emphasizes that. Note how he puts it about the dialogue: "All quotations [dialogue] . . . appear precisely as these individuals expressed them to me . . . ." It's as if we're sitting down with Uncle Silas, the noted family raconteur, and he starts: "The other day, I ran into Harry Emerald, you know, my old horse-playing buddy. Haven't seen him in years, and he says to me, 'Thought you was dead, but you look perky.' And I say, 'Stickin' to the clubhouse makes me happy, old friend.' He pokes me on the arm. 'Si, you fraud, the grandstand's where we used to *live!*' I give him a thumbs up: 'Never could fool you, Harry pal . . .'"

It's doubtful anyone would want to preserve these dialogue passages (or "quotations," to use Kurzman's approach) because they really don't push the story line along. But note where it leaves us: some "quotations" will work and some won't, and we have to decide which is which. Kurzman writes he didn't alter any quotations, and we should take him at his word, yet we also have to grapple with the question that arises where dialogue or "quotations" bog the story down. Should they be eliminated or truncated so only the most interesting parts remain? In other words can we "cherry pick" the quotations in order to rev up the story? Kurzman doesn't say, and we shouldn't make any assumptions other than to repeat his words: " . . . quotations . . . appear precisely as . . . expressed . . . ."

But any skillful writer knows that accurate quotes placed in dramatic order can accomplish a great deal so long as the salient facts aren't distorted. Leaving out passages that don't move the story along is what we as writers know how to do because we understand the demands of drama and what it has to accomplish. It's obvious that even following Kurzman's tight discipline about "quotations," we still have the flexibility to use some — dramatic! — dialogue passages, and not use others, all in the name of advancing the story.

Now take a look at the words of Joseph Wambaugh, who has become well known both for his fiction and for his nonfiction. His latter work has generally been in the true crime category, but this is nonfiction writing just as biography is nonfiction writing — both purport to provide an accurate, true story. Some years ago Joseph McGinnis wrote *Fatal Vision*, about the murder trial and conviction of Jeffrey MacDonald for killing his wife and two young children. Years later MacDonald sued McGinnis, claiming fraud in the way McGinnis obtained information from MacDonald about the crime. Journalist Janet Malcolm quoted some of the testimony in the trial, particularly Joseph Wambaugh who appeared in support of McGinnis and the way he dramatized the facts. Wambaugh stated:

> "When I write nonfiction, obviously I was
> not there when the events occurred. I write in a
> dramatic style — that is, I employ lots of dialogue,
> I describe feelings, I describe how the events must have

taken place. *I invent probable dialogue,
or at least possible dialogue based upon all of the
research I do . . .* (italics supplied)."

Note Joseph Wambaugh's differences with Dan Kurzman: where Kurzman claims he alters nothing in dialogue passages, Wambaugh says he "invents" dialogue if that suits his story. And he doesn't limit what he invents to a step below certainty; he says he even invents "possible" dialogue which, of course, opens a huge cavern of drama potential . . . as well as criticism. Which dialogue is "possible" becomes a relative thing, depending upon all the surrounding circumstances: for example, it might be "possible" to invent spontaneous dialogue reactions during the commission of a crime because there couldn't have been anything studied about it. But . . . how about "possible" dialogue in a corporate board meeting or a casual conversation on a crosstown bus? The point is that once we drop the barriers to some form of truthtelling, we're allowing the writer free imaginative reign, and when the standard is "possible" dialogue, haven't we come to the boundary of fiction? Possibilities, after all, are what fiction writers concern themselves with, and "possible" dialogue is exactly what most fiction writers seek to portray in their quest to involve the reader and provide a believable story.

Yet, strict quotation and "possible" dialogue are the opposite edges of the dialogue debate, and for most of us — and for most nonfiction writers — usual dialogue application falls somewhere in between. During the past forty years literary understanding has developed to the point where extended dialogue is permissible with nonfiction so long as the reader knows beforehand, and the writer doesn't become too greedy with dialogue invention.

Philip Gerard, in his *Creative Nonfiction,* puts it well: "The hitch," he writes, "about using dialogue in nonfiction is the obvious one: you can't make it up." It's a matter of obligation to the person being quoted as well as the reader, and the writer must be as accurate as he or she can be. But, he adds, there are two exceptions:

> "First, in memoir writing about remembered
> scenes, the writer usually has no choice but to
> re-create dialogue. You're trying to capture a flavor,
> to recover conversations long vanished into the ether . . . "

The reader, he believes, will be reasonable about this so long as the writer doesn't try to hide it and make it appear verbatim. The second exception to the accurate reproduction of dialogue standard is what he calls "habitual" dialogue, the "kind" of conversations the characters offer:

> "You're capturing the essence of the sort
> of talk that went on but you have to stop
> short of claiming that it actually happened . . . "

It's the type of dialogue that might spring from: "They used to sit around and talk about . . . " or "He remembered his mother and father would discuss the next day's weather at the dinner table . . . " For instance, it could go this way:

> Mom often sighed when she settled herself
> at the table. "Think it'll rain tomorrow, Jonas?"
> "Possible," Dad would answer, not looking
> up. "They're getting some right now over by Larned."
> "Doesn't mean we'll get it," Mom says.

"We could sure use it, though."
Mom looks up, and there's softness on her
face. "Never enough rain for you, Jonas . . . ."

Dialogue like this, under these circumstances, would pass muster with Philip Gerard because it's "habitual" in the sense that it was typical of what went on in that household on many evenings. No reader is going to expect verbatim transcript of words and phrases that he or she knows were repeated in similar form over and over.

Yet we can't simply present dialogue without molding it to accomplish certain goals. Novelist Anthony Trollope, many years ago, set the standard when he announced that all dialogue passages, even the smallest and shortest, must contribute to the telling of the story. For him needless words and phrases, even if an accurate portrayal of what was said, should not appear. It means that when a character answers the telephone, he or she doesn't have to say "hello!" or "goodbye." A simple launch into the meat of the conversation would be fine. For example, we have a scene and the telephone rings. The character picks up the receiver:

"Johnny . . . it's you!"
The voice on the other end is disembodied, a
gauzy, crinkly wheeze. "You got the money?"
"Tonight. Guaranteed . . . Johnny . . . ?"
"Better be." Slam! The line goes dead.

Not a word out of place here, everything moves the story along, and the drama is inherent in the confrontation. The dialogue is crisp, to the point, not a syllable just "hanging around." This is what Trollope meant, and this is what we should strive for.

And it doesn't matter whether it's fiction or nonfiction. So long as we remember the conventions already discussed, about accuracy of reproduction, alerting the reader to any "inventive" approach and maintaining a healthy sense of drama, our dialogue should add substantially to our story.

Even with nonfiction, dialogue can become art if we recognize its dramatic potential. A simple observation about the weather may not be much out of context, but provide it with connection to a character and it could take on new and more substantial meaning. How about this phrase: "a gray, frosty New England morning . . . "? By itself it offers a neutral weather observation, no excitement, no story. But put it into dialogue, and drama bursts forth:

> "Another goddam gray day," Jim spit out. "Even
> frost on the doorknob."
> "Wouldn't be if you'd put on the storm
> door," Marge said, pulling her sweater
> tighter.
> "I hate this weather!"
> "You hate everything . . . "

The drama seethes here, and if the characterizations are developed and the storyline moves forward, there could be artistry. Philip Gerard speaks of John McPhee's ability to create drama with his book on Alaska, *Coming Into the Country,* by juxtaposing several observations in dialogue about the same person, place or thing. What happens is the creation of a framework for artistry. Anyone of us can do it . . . :

> "Will the boat land on time?" I asked.

"Not this month," Maury said, turning to
light his cigarette.
"Got a new skipper," Jimmy added. "Fresh
out of one of them maritime schools."
"You gonna take the boat back?" Sonny wondered.
"Got a different schedule this year, you know,"
Jimmy said. "Must be somebody's idea . . . "

Now we have a scene that rings with conflict and the hint
of drama. By offering several different observations in answer
to a single question, we beef up the mood and develop an
image that puts us in the scene. The artistry comes by virtue
of the author's ability to create the image for us and to allow
us to enter the scene. It can be done solely through dialogue,
so long as we provide several observations in a row about a
single person, place or thing. Let the observations flow and
see the drama come alive!

Extended dialogue can also develop a single, full characterization by means of give and take between two persons.
The question isn't how many characters might be in a scene,
but how their dialogue is represented; in other words how
dramatically is it portrayed? We know what several observations about a single item can produce, so how about back-
and-forth observations on the same item?

In her 1978 book, *The Last Cowboy*, Jane Kramer portrays
Henry Blanton, a resident of the Texas panhandle, who has
worked with horses and cows his entire life. He is the embod-
iment of the "cowboy" myth, that relic of the nineteenth century which glorified the independent spirit, toughness and
love of the land that drove people to settle the western United
States. Kramer describes Henry Blanton this way: ". . . with
his horse under him and the range spread out around him,

[he] knew a truth and a freedom and a satisfaction that ordinary men did not."

But Henry Blanton's lifestyle is dying, and he's having difficulty adjusting to it. His father and his grandfather were cowboys, too, and Henry, now forty-one years old, is facing challenges from corporate ownership of the land and the animals his ancestors never had to experience. Kramer describes his attitudes and his working habits, and it's hard not to feel empathy for a man on the downslope of irrelevancy.

Yet the drama is more studied, less human than it needs to be . . . until Kramer relates the story of Henry, on his fortieth birthday, driving to town to celebrate with his brother, Tom, and describing a resolution he has just made:

> "It's like this, Tom," he said, after they had driven in silence for half an hour, passing Henry's pickup bottle back and forth. "Here I am getting a certain age, and I find I ain't accumulating nothing. I find . . . "
>
> Tom nodded.
>
> "I mean it was different with Daddy," Henry said. "Those old men like Daddy — they turned forty and they was just glad they had a job. But nowadays you turn forty — you figure you got ten, fifteen years left to really do something." Henry thought for awhile. "So that's what I'm figuring to do," he finally said. "Do something."
>
> "Shoot, Henry, we're just peons, you and me," said Tom.

Note the sense of inevitability here, the fact that these two brothers recognize they are incapable of altering or stopping the changes that are coming. Henry at least feels spurred to action (he wants to "do something"), but Tom has no illusions that they could make any difference (we're just peons"), and in this dichotomy of reactions we see the drama of the situation played out. They are both reacting to the same link of events — inevitable changes in the way they will live and work — but it is in their different reactions that we find the drama, and that's because they portray opposite sides of the same dilemma. Do I fight it . . . do I go along with it . . . and how long have I got before I have to decide?

In many ways it's a conflict situation over and over, and as we've seen repeatedly, conflict is the truest spur for drama. It is in the confrontation of people, events and/or circumstances that we end up taking sides and rooting. Every writer hopes to develop his or her story to this point . . . so the reader can become a *part* of it all because once that is achieved, interest and attention is focused and rarely lost.

See what Jane Kramer has done here, using dialogue. She has portrayed the different sides of an ages-old dilemma: do we fight the monster of progress or do we step aside because there isn't much we can do anyway? She uses a simple technique: the same issue, two different attitudes. The inherent conflict in viewpoint sparks the drama, but portrayal through dialogue is what adds poignancy and image-making. Can't we picture Henry, taking a slug of whiskey, wiping his mouth, weathered gaze on the road ahead, voice even . . . "So that's what I'm figuring to do . . . Do something."

He's an anachronism, he knows it, and he's not going to sit still about it.

Only . . . he has no idea what to do.

The image grows clear, and somehow we find ourselves rooting for him.

The Last Cowboy. He might well be that!

5.

Clues, Hints, Signs

We've all had a taste of it, that crushing moment when we're with a person we care about, *really* care about, and the words come tumbling at us . . . "over" . . . "finished" . . . "stop seeing" . . . "go separate ways" . . .

Maybe we knew it was coming, but the finality catches us off guard, because we never expected things to peter down like the sputtering of an old sewing machine.

Then or later, perhaps, we'll look back and ask . . . could things have worked out differently if we'd seen it coming?

Were there clues, hints, signs?

If we're honest, we'll admit — to ourselves, anyway — there probably were indications, though self-purging like this is never easy.

But the point is no relationship atomizes from a healthy level; there has to be some erosion, subtle or not, infecting the whole. It is this erosion that brings about the demise of the relationship, and it is the erosion or the effects of it that some of us fail to pick up.

Hints . . . signs . . . clues . . . these are the subtle ways we communicate with one other, and sometimes they are more meaningful than direct conversation. For example, a man buys flowers for his wife's birthday, but by the time he gives them to her they have lost their freshness. "Honey," he says, "I was so busy I knew I wouldn't have time to buy them, so I got them yesterday . . . ."

The wife has two choices: "It's the thought, that's what counts," or recognize that one can *always* find time to buy flowers . . . if one really wants to!

In the latter case, of course, the result is to focus upon not what was said, but what was *meant*, and that puts a much different slant on how the relationship plays. In a very real sense the husband is tipping off his feelings by the way he treats his wife's birthday, and eventually things will end badly for them unless they work out their difficulties.

What the husband is doing by offering such an excuse is foreshadowing not only his feelings but his ultimate actions. He's letting us in on his attitude toward his wife, and this would be true *even if he wasn't aware of it!* Is it such a jump to imagine his disdain for her growing in the coming months until they both realize there's nothing left? Does the foreshadowing represent an important event in the demise of their relationship?

Yes, of course, once we establish that the relationship is going to fail. Then the foreshadowing has real meaning because it's given us an early clue as to what will happen later.

And whether the subject is the soap-opera life of friends or a literary presentation, the ability to pick up on a clue, a hint or a sign presents us with an opportunity to sense now what could happen later. That doesn't mean, of course, that it will happen, only that it *could* happen.

And in real life or in a work of literature that's enough to keep our attention.

The device of foreshadowing is clearly a basic drama technique in fiction (think of Desdemona's dropped handkerchief in *Othello* or Queeg rolling his steel balls in *The Caine Mutiny* — both foreshadow disaster!). But the same technique can work with nonfiction, as well, and it doesn't even have to be particularly subtle!

Take a look at *Rude Awakening,* the story of the rise, fall and rise of General Motors in the final decade and a half of the twentieth century, by Maryann Keller. She details the fascinating interplay between GM Chairman Roger Smith and H. Ross Perot, whose Electronics Data Systems was bought by GM for 2.5 billion dollars. As part of the price, Perot joined the GM Board of Directors, and his entrepreneurial, down-to-earth style immediately conflicted with the collegial, elitist style that GM espoused. Several years before Perot came on the scene, one of GM's many management committees discovered it was taking longer to bring a car from idea to showroom than it took to win World War II. Keller writes:

"It was a line that was to be often repeated by
H. Ross Perot in his criticism of GM."

Perot's name did not surface in the text for quite a while after this single reference, yet now we're alerted to his inclusion in the story and to the fact he will play a conflicted role somewhere down the line.

In 1986 GM bought EDS, agreeing that EDS should remain a separate entity and profit center within the GM corporate structure. Keller alludes once again to the coming struggle

"But as Roger Smith and Ross Perot were shaking

hands on what they billed as a synergistic relationship, each man perceived reality in a different way. Smith believed he could bring Ross Perot into his camp as a team player . . . . Perot, on the other hand, believed that he could infuse GM with the messianic zeal he had brought to EDS . . . ."

Then, in the very next sentence, Keller underscores her foreshadowing:

"The rude awakening would come before the marriage was even consummated . . . ."

Within weeks trouble broke out as GM and EDS employees traded barbs and criticisms and then made them public. It was a culture clash that interfered with the respective businesses and brought minimal cooperation from each side. In the end it was clear the divide between Perot and the GM way of doing things was simply too vast to be reconstructed. GM could go only one way — they made Perot an offer he couldn't refuse, and Perot sold his GM stock back to the company and walked away, leaving Roger Smith to answer some tough questions from GM stockholders.

What Keller shows here is that we needn't assume foreshadowing must be carried out with subtlety. Certainly, hinting and indirection are classic ways for developing foreshadowing, but sometimes — as here — a more direct approach works just as well.

Ask ourselves this question: what do we want to accomplish with our hinting, our clues, our signs? Generally, we're trying to inject dramatic appeal into our story, and foreshadowing offers sinister uncertainty which the reader can sense will have *some,* as yet undetermined, effect. What grabs the reader is the mystery, the uncertainty, of how it will play out.

And because the reader is caught up in the mystery, we have their attention and, hence, their interest.

So, when Maryann Keller writes about the impending culture clash between GM and EDS and tells us about the differing assumptions of Roger Smith and Ross Perot, she's foreshadowing the eruption in the way a good nonfiction writer would: with facts and truths, letting them speak for themselves because there was more than enough drama to go around. She didn't need to be subtle or hint about their conflict — all she needed was to alert us it was bound to happen, and the dramatic impact would take place.

The same type of approach can take place on a much smaller stage. Foreshadowing in a simple article or personal essay could follow the same format — a straightforward statement that an unpleasant or conflict-laden situation was coming up. Suppose we want to show the preparations an over-confident mountain climber makes for a perilous climb. We already know the ultimate storyline: the climber will not survive and we've researched the entire event, but how do we foreshadow — or present clues — about it?

Because of the danger and drama inherent in mountain climbing we don't need to beef things up with "technique" beyond the simple statement:

> "Jim believed his superior physical strength
> could rescue him from any tight situation,
> so he laughed off the suggestion he pack a
> third safety line. It would cost him dearly . . . ."

It is the last line, *It would cost him dearly* . . . that gives us the clue, and as we see it isn't especially subtle or indirect. But it does give us a hint that something unforeseen and deadly will probably happen.

Do we need more?

Isn't the reader sufficiently aroused to the possibility now without another dose of drama?

Shouldn't we leave it right here for the time being?

If you answer no . . . yes . . . yes . . . I agree.

In her book, *Writing and Reporting News*, journalist Carole Rich speaks about using narrative for an article's lead sentence as the foreshadowing mechanism. " . . . A narrative lead tells a story," she writes. "It relates the story or reconstructs the incident so the readers can feel as if they are witnessing it. Narrative writing uses all the techniques of fiction, including dialogue, scene setting and foreshadowing — giving clues to what will happen . . . ."

She describes an article by Nancy Weil about an early morning robbery at a convenience store that appeared in the *St. Petersburg (Florida) Times* a few years ago. The article begins:

> "It was a little past 2:30 A.M. at the Circle K
> and the 35 year old woman on duty was alone.
> Her terror was about to begin . . ."

The last sentence is the foreshadowing, and clearly it is neither subtle nor indirect. The author doesn't sneak up by writing:

> "She didn't like being alone at night because
> strange things might happen . . ."

Or:

"It would be an unforgettable night . . ."

Instead, she writes the clerk is about to face terror, and she will tell us about it. Call this "direct" foreshadowing if you like, because it doesn't beat about the bush with hints or indirections. But it serves the purpose of building uncertainty in that while we know something will happen, we don't know what it will be.

By contrast, when we use "indirect" foreshadowing where hints and indirections are, there is essentially a two-step process: we don't know whether something will happen (because the hints may not be picked up or if picked up, may not be followed) AND even if we come to accept that something will happen, we still don't know what it will be.

"Indirect" foreshadowing might include an oblique reference to the weather:

"He hoped the day wouldn't prove stormy
as the clouds gathered . . ."

Or it might be something to do with one's mental state:

"He felt a strange wariness as the forest
shadows began to lengthen . . ."

Or it might be something to do with time:

"Three hours, fifty minutes, before the last
boat left; he was sure he'd finish before then . . ."

Each of these gives a hint that something might happen, but none of them offer the certainty that it *will* happen.

Contrast this with the story by Nancy Weil above. She writes: "Her terror was about to begin . . . ." There's no uncertainty here, no subtlety, we're clear the terror *will* happen.

When do we use "direct" foreshadowing, and when do we rely on "indirect" use? It's more a question of style and the type of writing we're producing. As a general rule, this might suffice: the more fact-oriented our work and the less reliance we place on fiction-oriented devices for dramatic impact, the more appropriate it would be to use "direct" foreshadowing. Conversely, the more we use drama build-up devices such as quick scene cuts or development of sensory perceptions, the more we should turn to "indirect" foreshadowing. In other words the closer we approach to using fiction technique the more indirection, hinting and subtle foreshadowing should we use. The reason's fairly clear: if we're laying out the facts in orderly fashion, dramatic though they may be, why change the pace by trying to be subtle? We run the risk of confusing the reader as well as breaking up the continuity and clarity of our prose.

Alternatively, if we're trying to polish the facts so they provide a more interesting, more dramatic story, wouldn't we also use whatever dramatic technique would be available to us? If subtlety, indirection and hinting add zest to our story by providing dramatic oomph with foreshadowing, so be it.

Take a look at this approach to foreshadowing by essayist Andre Dubus in his short work, "Witness." In the opening he gives some facts about himself which, at first glance, seem clear and unambiguous. He narrates that he picks up his daughters each week at their private school and drives them to his house for dinner. He describes himself as spending a lot of time in a wheelchair. He writes in the opening paragraph:

"My right leg hurts when I drive; it hurts when
it is not at a ninety-degree angle, and most nights
it hurts anyway . . . . Years ago I learned that pain and
wheelchair fatigue — sitting and worrying about
what can go wrong because I can't stand or
walk — take most of my energy."

At this point most of us would think he's characterizing himself for us, providing information so we can come to know him better, as he moves toward making his point with the essay. It's doubtful many would catch the idea it was really foreshadowing, yet that's exactly what it is because later on he happens to meet — fortuitously — someone who witnessed the event that put him in the wheelchair and then we come to understand the trauma he underwent which put him in constant pain. Reliving the event years later somehow gives him a measure of peace.

Would we pick up on this from the opening? He doesn't tell us how he got injured or even that his disability was the result of an accident; all he does is describe his pain, his weekly dinner with his daughters and his physical limitations. We want to know what happened, but his style is such that the how and why seem downplayed, even though later they become crucial. He's hinting here, not shouting, "PAY ATTEN-TION! I'm letting you in on my disability so that later you can appreciate what it's done for my character . . . ."

Quite obviously, this is "indirect" foreshadowing because he's not telling us, at least not in the beginning, the how and why of his disability, and we're left to wonder about it. Eventually it all comes out, as it should, but the uncertainty of the how and why is one of the things that hold us to the page. And that's the effect of "indirect" foreshadowing.

The marvelous Russian short-story writer Anton Chekov offers a foreshadowing tip that all nonfiction writers should remember. He may have had fiction writing in mind, but his advice works just as well with nonfiction. "If, in the first chapter, you say there is a gun hanging on the wall," he writes, "you should make quite sure that it is going to be used further in the story." His point is simply that the writer needs to play fair with the reader. If something sinister or unusual or attention-grabbing appears in the early part of the story, the chances are you've aroused the curiosity of the reader who's looking for some explanation about why that item was there. If we don't satisfy that curiosity at some point in the story, the reader is not going to be happy, and that will reflect in the way the reader characterizes the story to others.

So, foreshadow wherever and whenever you like, but remember! What you foreshadow needs to be dealt with at some point later on. Don't assume the reader wasn't paying attention or didn't catch the significance.

John McPhee is a master at developing his storylines and using clues, hints and signs. In a book-length manuscript the opportunities to foreshadow are much more numerous than with a short piece of work, but that doesn't change the rules — the writer must still tie things up, somehow. McPhee can take a complicated subject and lay it out for us in dramatic fashion so that we can be caught up in the struggle or the quest or the survival of his protagonists. What he puts on the page actually happens or has happened, but how he presents it is where his skill comes in.

Take a look at his book, *Looking For a Ship*, the story of Andy Chase from Maine who holds a second mate's license in the U.S. Merchant Marine and seeks to sign on with a ship out of one of the east coast ports. Andy is a member of the

International Organization of Masters, Mates and Pilots which controls, through seniority, who sails on which ship. All hiring is done through the union hall, and Andy decides to go to Charleston, South Carolina, because there will be less competition there for the available slots. McPhee describes the scene in the union hall where a clipboard with a sheaf of papers headed "Offshore Jobs" lists positions recently filled. He reads where the ships were bound: "Coastwise" . . . "Far East" . . . "South America" . . . "N. Europe" . . . "W. Africa . . . "Med" . . . and then he writes:

> "Andy said, 'South America is the romance run —
> beautiful women, beautiful ports.' Andy had never
> been to South America . . . ."

His first day in Charleston, Andy finds out two ships will be leaving for Europe shortly, while a third, the *SS Stella Lykes,* will be sailing for South America in two weeks. He chooses those going on the Europe run, and puts his name in the hat. You never let an opportunity go by, he tells McPhee, but while he was waiting to see if his seniority would get him aboard, he realized there wouldn't be a lot of sea time on either ship. And what he needed was sea time if he was to stand for a Chief Mate's exam at some point in the future.

He turns his attention to the *Stella Lykes,* and McPhee writes:

> "The Stella Lykes was the most appealing ship.
> Second mate. Interesting run. All the sea time he
> wanted and needed. But to wait for the Stella Lykes
> meant weeks, not days, multiplying the possibility
> that something could go wrong . . . ."

Andy decides to take a chance on the *Stella Lykes*, and he spends the next two weeks doing piece work and waiting . . .

Nine pages later, McPhee writes:

> "At eleven forty-five in the union hall, a sheet went up on the board . . . SHIP . . . SS Stella Lykes . . . The telephone rang at one thirty-one. [Andy's wife] was calling from Maine. Yes. Andy had a ship: the Stella Lykes . . . ."

Here is classic application of Chekov's rule: mention a gun in chapter one, and you better use it somewhere later on. Note McPhee mentions South America when Andy first arrives at the union hall. Andy calls South America "the romance run," and that's all McPhee writes. He doesn't embellish Andy's comment, nor does he try to highlight it. He writes it as an offhand comment in the midst of other casual conversation at the union hall. But South America has been mentioned, it's on the table, and Andy has gone so far as to sound enthusiastic about the possibility.

So a good writer — as John McPhee certainly is — wouldn't let it sit without some use later on. And that's precisely what happens when Andy decides he'll take his chance on the *Stella Lykes*, even though someone with more seniority might come in at the last moment and whisk the opportunity away from him. The foreshadowing comes full circle when Andy does get the ship and is on the "romance run" to South America. In Chekov's words, the gun has now been properly used.

6.

Where Am I?

Imagine reading Henry David Thoreau without visualizing his lonely encampment on the shores of Walden Pond . . . or Ernest Hemingway's prowls through African landscape without sensing the vastness that he relished . . . or the memoirs of Henry Kissinger without picturing the carefully crafted relationships that create a personal mood and atmosphere behind White House walls.

There's uniqueness in these viewpoints because they represent a single individual's personal assessment of his or her surroundings. In this we see the development of what writers call "a sense of place," an image of where we are as the story unfolds. A few years ago I wrote *Three Rules For Writing A Novel,* and while the book dealt with fiction, the basic principles apply to nonfiction, too.

Three rules, that's all:

— what's happening?
— who am I?
— where am I?

The first two concern plotting and character development. But the third — where am I? — that's our sense of place. Without it, we're doomed to write a story that meanders to nowhere . . . an inter-planetary creature without home or family.

And the reader? Equally unfixed because they rely on us to tie things down.

If it's story-telling we're after, then the type of writing — fiction or nonfiction — doesn't matter. The important thing is to get the reader's feet on firm ground, some place that's clearly defined, so a base for story development can come about. For example, if we're describing a rarely seen animal, we can take pages discussing the creature's characteristics — color, size, mating habits — those individual items that give us an image of shape and dimension. But until we talk about where the animal is found, how it sustains itself and what lifestyle it enjoys we can't appreciate its rooted permanence. It is simply two-dimensional until this time. The sense of place fills in crevasses on the plain of reality, thus making the picture more complete.

Look at it this way: we could write of such an animal:

"It carries a coat of gray with a single
black stripe down the middle of its back,
its pig-like snout continually vacuuming
critters from the thick grass . . ."

This provides an image of the animal, but isn't it little more than a wall painting? We need to ask the basic question: where am I? Only then can we flesh out the animal and provide a third dimension.

Suppose we write:
"As dusk comes he searches out

already-marked abandoned dens,
preferring used spaces to anything
he might develop on his own. He's the
squatter champ of East Africa . . ."

Now we have a sense of place because we know where this animal likes to nest and what he seeks for living accommodation. His sense of place is clear: someone else's abandoned digs.

We may find the animal's sense of place unappetizing, but that's not the point. When we ask, where am I! we're seeking more than imagery, we're seeking knowledge.

Identifying this — or any other — sense of place is not the end of our portrayal, however. We can know where our story will take place, but the real task is to make that place vibrant and alive for the reader. Developing the "sense" of that place both in our characters and in the reader is what we strive to do because only then can our story be fleshed out. Only then can it have substance and heft.

The emphasis is on "sense," not place, because we're trying to touch the reader's emotional commitment to where our story occurs. If we write: "This story happens in Baltimore . . ." and then add a string of city characteristics such as crabcakes, baseball, fine medical schools . . . , we have place identification, but the "sense" of it isn't there.

And if the "sense" isn't there, then understanding and identification with the characters will fall away because everything will remain two-dimensional.

So we have to add that third dimension to put "sense" in sense of place and hook the reader emotionally.

David Fryxell, nonfiction editor for *Writer's Digest Magazine,* offers one idea on establishing a sense of art in an article, "Paint a picture in words." He suggests the use of image-provoking words to convey the feelings and the vibrancy of the place where our story is set.

Don't list what novelist Arturo Vivante, in another context, calls "passport details" — name, size, colors, dimensions, founding dates, famous citizens . . . these might work for the almanac, but they won't work in dramatic nonfiction.

Think about the "sense" of a place, its emotional content and connections, its effect on the characters and how they deal with it. An excruciating example of just this can be found in John Hersey's masterful yet unnerving short work, *Hiroshima,* about the personal aftermath of suffering and sorrow in the wake of the atomic bomb explosion in early August, 1945. Instead of offering "passport" details, Hersey focuses on Dr. Sasaki, the lone, uninjured doctor at the Red Cross Hospital, and he describes the doctor's world in the midst of the death and destruction:

> " . . . he began to find dreadful burns. He realized then
> that casualties were pouring in from outdoors. There
> were so many that he began to pass up the lightly
> wounded, he decided that all he could hope to do
> was to stop people from bleeding to death . . ."

He goes on to describe wounded, bleeding people filling every open spot in and around the building, including the streets leading to the hospital, and he adds: ". . . disfigured families leaned together. Many people were vomiting . . . ."

Here, then, out of the horror and chaos, is a grotesque sense of place. Note that Hersey doesn't write in panoramic terms listing the number of victims, how much of the city was reduced to rubble and what the general political status had become. Instead, he zeroes in on one man, and by painting the horror around him, he provides the sense of overwhelming disaster facing this lone survivor as he tries to cope . . . and ultimately the total disaster throughout the city.

The sense of place is horrific to be sure, but then, that's what really happened, and since this is nonfiction we have to stay within the facts. What Hersey shows is that this shouldn't present a major hurdle to an accomplished writer. He "paints a picture in words" as David Fryxell advises, and he does so in stark terms that become embedded in our consciousness. He offers this sense of place artistically and thoroughly, and anyone reading this entire account could easily feel the doomsday effect of what he has written.

Setting such a horrific scene may not work for all writers. Squeamishness or distaste or simple disinterest may block off a desire to create this world, and that's simply a matter of choice. There are, to be sure, myriad ways to develop that appropriate sense of place, and one shouldn't get bogged down pursuing a method that doesn't fit well.

For example, many writing teachers use the technique of the SINGLE BIG DETAIL when they ask writing students to sketch a set scene. It could be a single room or a parking lot or a group of runners or even a covey of animals. The point is to train the writer's eye so the most important detail in the scene is highlighted. The hope is that the detail highlighted will convey strong enough mood and atmosphere to carry the story along.

Why not single out several details so more ground could be covered? Think of adding water to unbeaten eggs readied for an omelet. A little water is ok, but add a half dozen spoonfuls, and suddenly nothing will set up, the omelet won't bind, and we'll have a mess on our hands.

Focusing on several details in a scene has the same effect. The overall dramatic effect is diluted because no one detail will stand out. Then, the scene itself will fall apart because there's no drama to keep it going.

The SINGLE BIG DETAIL works well with "where am I?" providing the detail is carefully chosen and the writer doesn't expect it to do more than it can. For example, if we're writing a story about mollusk-searching off the coast of St. Malo, France, during low tide, we should know that these are among the strongest, largest tides in the world. When they reverse, they start moving at about two inches per minute, and an unwary mollusk-searcher could easily get into trouble. Writing about the mollusks may be the thrust of the piece, but the SINGLE BIG DETAIL has to be the sinister nature of the tides, and this is what we emphasize to provide our sense of place:

> Staring at scooped-out mollusk sandholes
> alongside a rock should not consume one's
> attention. There! a tiny rivulet of sea slides
> about the rock, then pumps up and over. In
> a moment mollusks that were ready for harvesting
> are tucked in an unreachable cocoon until the
> next tidal change . . .

This single detail stays in the forefront of the story throughout, and it provides the major source of drama: danger, danger, danger . . . never let your mind wander far from the tides!

The SINGLE BIG DETAIL characterizes nonfiction writing well because, just as with fiction, we're seeking dramatic impact. Note the following excerpt from Sara Davidson's *Real Property* where she describes front yards of various single apartments in a nearby building. She notes tenants tend to stay only six months, and she can tell where they are in the cycle by the way their front yards look:

> "If there is a new resident in the building, the yard
> is full of young plants. They are carefully watered
> and begin to flower and then overnight everything
> turns brown. Weeds spring up until the ground is
> so dry that nothing will grow on it and people
> throw beer cans and trash on the lot . . . ."

The old tenants move on and new ones begin the process all over again. "I watch them installing stereos, hanging wind-chimes and putting out lawn furniture. Home at last . . . ."

The sense of place she gives us is one of transience and impermanence, a place where no one stays very long but where the urge to nest-build blooms . . . until the notion of impermanence takes over. Note she uses the SINGLE BIG DETAIL — the state of the front yard — to give us insight into the nature of the apartment building and the tenants, and this provides a base for whatever story will follow. Carry it a step or two further: impermanence will influence the way characters deal with one another, with the way repairs to the building are made, with the very nature of the relationships inside the building. Impermanence will control the storyline, and we need look no further than sense of place to see it develop.

Sometimes, of course, there is no SINGLE BIG DETAIL for the sense of place to fasten upon. Suppose we want to set the story in a Costa Rican rain forest, and we want to establish the vibrance of the living organisms there. Because there are literally thousands of such creatures, choosing one and then further choosing one significant detail of the organism's lifestyle in order to pursue the SINGLE BIG DETAIL theory isn't enough. The mosaic is too big, too vast, too complicated to work well. To give an adequate sense of place for the rain forest would require meshing a number of details about different organisms so that a multi-layered sense of place would emerge. We might come away with a single image — life can be dangerous in the rain forest, for example — but it will be made from a series of details.

This is exactly the way it comes together for Richard West in a piece he did some years ago for *New York Magazine*. He called it "The Power of 21" and it was about "21" restaurant, the famous New York City landmark. In the first few pages he describes how well-known customers are treated, what they eat, where they sit, how long they have been coming. Basically, these are "passport" details because they merely show us the restaurant is exclusive, expensive and well attended. A number of other New York restaurants could make the same claims, so the sense of place at "21" — at this point — is not special. Anyone who has eaten in an expensive New York restaurant would be on familiar territory here, and this doesn't make it more or less interesting for us.

But remember this is "21" we're talking about, and the writer knew there was more here than just an upscale expensive, exclusive, well-attended restaurant. Therefore, he dug a bit further, observed a bit more, and he was able to offer a sense of place for "21" that put it in a different — and special — category. Midway in his piece, he writes:

"There are more formal rules of the house: coats
and knotted ties required (but shoes without socks
permitted); dark suits after six encouraged; photograph
taking forbidden; children in the bar after six

discouraged; seating requests for up or downstairs
permitted; tables never promised except to a
select few . . . During the 1930s [the owner] waived
the no-woman-in-pants rule for Katherine Hepburn
but no one else . . ."

Clearly, what we have here is a restaurant so well controlled that a rigorous dress code and parental responsibility
are enforced, and in these rules is the essence of the sense of
place that "21" projects. There's no SINGLE, BIG DETAIL
here, but there sure are a lot of little details, and when we
combine them, we come away with an image of exclusivity
bolstered by a no-nonsense policy of serious purpose. This is
a special restaurant, say the rules, it's not a place for your
child after dark, it's not a place for celebrity-hawking, it's not
a place where you can buy your way to a preferred table.

It is, however, a place where you will be well cared for IF
you've been coming for awhile and you've stayed within the
rules. "21" works because we're careful here, and we expect
you to understand that.

A special place, different from other New York exclusive,
expensive restaurants, because it projects itself that way.

A well-defined sense of place to be sure.

Sometimes it isn't overt rules that develop "where am I?"
Rather, it can be exposure to a different set of customs or
habits that paint an unusual picture. Something memorable
and different which gives character and imagery? Norman
Sims wrote about this in a book he edited, *The Literary
Journalists,* where he says that nonfiction writers ". . . bring
themselves into their stories to greater or lesser degrees and
confess to human failings and emotions. Through their eyes
we watch ordinary people in crucial contexts . . . these

authors understand and convey feeling and emotion, the inner dynamics of culture . . . ."

What he's saying is that the "sense" of the sense of place can be based upon the feelings and emotions engendered by the nature of the cultural context. For example, in many Latin communities inside or outside the United States, a dinner invitation simply assumes the children will accompany the adults, that an evening's socializing includes all, even toddling, children. So, a writer describing such an evening must make allowance for the presence of children in the scene. The "sense" of such a place is that adults and children intermingle and the feelings and emotions of the characters, which the writer must portray, play off that.

Take this scene from a Portuguese colonial household that I have personally experienced:

The dinner table is strewn with bamboo serving dishes, and the gamy flavor of goat hangs in the air. Arturo looks at his young son who has been in a staring contest with a cousin across the table.

"Ho, boy, put some of that good food on your plate . . ."

He turns to me, laughing. "The boy tried his hand at the goat-slaughter, today, and his belly . . . well . . . not so good!" Arturo reaches into a pocket of his *guyabara.* "Here, boy!"

He offers a shriveled sliver of softened sinew, graying, formless about three inches long.
"Take it," he orders, "keep close to the heart."

Then to me: "Goat's prong, it will push his manhood . . ."

The sense of place here is the cultural strangeness — to us — of a family feasting on goat meat and the father using the occasion to pump up the son's virile self-image. Not only must the boy slaughter the goat and be prepared to eat the meat (which, by the way, is never eaten right after slaughter. As with beef, goat's meat must be aged for several weeks at least, so I assume the meat we were served was not the goat that was slaughtered earlier that day), but the boy must consider the dead goat's penis a talisman to promote and sustain his manhood.

The cultural context may be offensive to some, but there's no denying the "sense" of the place where this dinner took place. The father, Arturo, is clearly an overwhelming presence in his family, and life inside the household reflects that. There's an obvious strain of macho paternalism, but it's also reflective of the Latin approach to children: they are important enough to be included in most basic rites of family life (such as slaughtering and gathering food) and to be offered traditional charms to ensure a better life.

It is with unfamiliar customs and habits that a meaningful sense of place can emerge. Our imaginations blossom, and we have little trouble placing ourselves within the scene. We come to "understand" and then we read on.

Take a look at the way Maxine Hong Kingston describes, in "Catfish in the Bathtub," what she had to contend with when she had dinner in her Chinese-American family. The family's diet was varied, to say the least; her mother cooked — and the family ate — raccoon, skunk, hawks, snakes, garden snails, domesticated turtles and catfish that swam in the bathtub. But it was something else that she remembers most vividly:

"In a glass jar on a shelf my mother kept a big
brown hand with pointed claws stewing in

alcohol and herbs. She must have brought it
from China because I do not remember a
time when I did not have the hand to look at.
She said it was a bear's claw, and for many
years I thought bears were hairless. My
mother used the tobacco, leeks and grasses
swimming about the hand to rub our sprains . . . "

Here, then, are customs that many of us have little knowledge about. Bear claws in alcohol . . . raccoons and skunks on the dinner table . . . living like this might seem grotesque to the more conventional among us, but that's not the point. The writer is developing a sense of place that's vivid enough to snare our imaginations and sturdy enough to support the story she wants to tell. Quite obviously she's off to a good start, and the lesson for us is this: unfamiliar habits and customs are a good springboard for answering the question, where am I?, and if the underlying story has substance, there's a solid foundation to move everything forward.

One of the more effective ways to set a scene is to highlight details that stand in opposition to one another. A kind of ying and yang approach where the nature of the conflict paints the sense of place and provides juxtaposed tranquillity. For example, writers on the Viet Nam conflict such as Michael Herr and Philip Caputo could describe the shrieking chaos of war — shell-bursting, smoke-gagging, jet-whining — and reach out to portray soldiers exchanging family photos. We get both extremities of the scene: destruction and preservation, and somewhere in the middle is the sense of place.

Where am I? On a battlefield filled with death, but by God, I'm not going to lose *all* my humanity! I have my feelings and emotions, and no one's going to suck those out of me!

The sense of place, then, is this: dangerous, sometimes overwhelming, but with room — still — for a vibrant human touch.

Opposites abound in our world: cruelty and kindness, beauty and ugliness, generosity and greed.

Take very large and very small . . . these opposites can provide a vivid sense of place by nature of the paradox they induce: the huge ship and the tiny sailboat, the seven-foot man and the midget, the skillful acrobat and the clumsy stagehand. The point is that if both extremes appear in the same scene, they represent the so-called ying and yang of the sense of place. Where am I? On the high seas fearful my small sailboat will be swamped by the bow wave of the ocean liner . . . or on a front porch chuckling at how a man half his size can order a giant about . . . or under an empty circus tent where the performer and the stagehand are working out a new routine.

The sense of place is not the "place" itself — the front porch, for example — but the "sense" that develops there, too. So, with the giant and the midget we sense the compatibility between them, and we understand they are a unit. To climb into their world we need to know that, and then we understand what they might do or say. We have come to recognize their sense of place.

Paul Theroux portrays this type of approach well in *The Old Patagonia Express,* his book about riding the train from Boston to the tip of South America. The last stage of the journey is to Esquel in southernmost Patagonia, and the train deposits him late at night in this end-of-the-line town with its one-story houses and one-roomed huts and road turning into a dusty track to nowhere. There was, he writes:

" . . . a rocky slope, some sheep, the rest bushes and

weeds. If you looked closely, you could see small pink and yellow flowers on these bushes. The wind stirred them. I went closer. They shook. But they were pretty. Behind my head was a great desert."

He then speaks of the paradox of opposites:

" . . . to be here, it helped to be a miniaturist, or else interested in enormous empty spaces.There was no intermediate zone of study.. Either the enormity of the desert space or the sight of a tiny flower. You had to choose between the tiny or the vast."

The tiny or the vast. Opposites. What do they project about the sense of place?

Perhaps it's this: even in a barren world a bit of beauty can shine, that space is merely a vessel in which the extremes of the environment can survive. Vast or tiny, it doesn't matter, our sense of place tells us we're in the midst of a paradox no different than cruising the ocean on a small sailboat and coming upon an unseeing behemoth of an ocean liner.

Let the paradox stand. Where am I? Wherever my sense of place has deposited me.

7.

Create That Flashback!

We think of time in two ways: a measure of where we are and a measure of where we've been. (Futurists will add a third category: a measure of where we will be.) Writing in the present is our starting point because this is our essential reality, and all else — forward and back — proceeds from what we perceive as appropriate for readers *now*! Offering a tale to contemporary readers written in seventeenth century English might be a *tour de force* among the literary elite, but most writers would turn away because their readers would turn away. Similiarly, conjuring a tale in a style that two hundred years from now readers might be comfortable with carries the same flaws. We write for readers *today* even if our stories jump backwards or forwards, and we use time as a place-setter, not as a world-creator. For example, we can write of George Washington and his army crossing the Delaware River on Christmas morning 1776 and winning a battle, but we wouldn't write the story as an eighteenth-century writer would. We'd write in a style and with language appropriate to today!

Yet the concept of time must be harnessed by all writers to

give life to the writing. We must understand that time is not a static event, it moves forward or backward, never still, always in motion like the ever-flowing river. Time gives us perspective because it provides dimension and substance for the story we're writing. Try this little experiment: write one paragraph on a truly sad moment in your life, and see if time can be kept out of the narrative and the story remain vibrant. If we don't offer when or relate it to some other event in our lives, the story falls flat because it simply hangs out there unconnected. But if we add some element of time such as "it was a cold dreary November day" or "I was fourteen when it happened," the entire story becomes more comprehensible.

Time, then, works for us as we write our stories. "I remembered his smile as if it had been eleven years ago, and we had just finished the race." Or "Three hours earlier he had been at the party when Gwen dropped the book on the table . . . ."

Most of us know this type of device as a flashback, and it uses time as a place-setter for a portion of the overall story. Note I use "portion" because few stories work well if they depend entirely on flashbacks. But as a way of fleshing out additional aspects to a story or providing more detailed insights, flashbacks are valuable, not only because they add substance to a story but also because they can add dramatic push to the events.

For example, a character confronted by a challenge is confused about which way to proceed. He thinks and thinks . . . and finally remembers a similiar event some years earlier . . . and suddenly we're in a flashback as he goes over his step-by-step procedure for resolving the dilemma then, and how he can apply it all now. The flashback takes him back, and the solution brings him forward to the present.

Rita Berman in her 1997 piece, "Creative Nonfiction

Writing," calls flashbacks a fiction-writer's device that can be applied to nonfiction. "By means of the flashback," she writes, "you can expand your story and take the reader into a direction different from where you began."

She's on the money here because we're using time to set a new place — one that occurs in the past. See how essayist Andre Dubus does it in his piece, "Witness," where he talks of the physical disability which confines him to a wheelchair and the pain and discomfort that accompany him every day. Then, near the end of the piece, he writes of a chance meeting with a woman he's never seen before:

> "The woman came to me, looking down now at my face. She said, 'I've been wanting to talk to you for some time. I saw your accident.'
> 'You did?'
> 'I was with my friend at the call box.'
> Ten years, three months, and one day before this lovely October afternoon, between midnight and one in the morning. on I-93 north of Boston , I saw a car stopped on a highway . . . "

He describes getting out to help and being hit by a speeding vehicle. He relates the conversation about his accident with the woman and relives the incident. But note how he gets into the flashback. He uses dialogue to precipitate it:

> " . . . I saw your accident . . . "

Three lines farther down, he writes:
> "Ten years, three months . . . "

Dialogue isn't the first line of the flashback, but it's what catalyzes the time sequence. The dialogue leads to the flashback which then proceeds in narrative form. See how he uses time: "Ten years, three months . . . " and now we have a place-setter for the story to continue. Imagine trying to do this without some reference to *when* the event occurred. If we leave off the time reference and begin "I saw a car stopped on the highway . . . " we'd be adrift in uncertainty, and the story, itself, would lose credibility and substance. Questions of relevance would arise: how does this tie in?

But once we tie the flashback to a definite time sequence, we have a platform from which to proceed. And as we see, it operates with nonfiction as well as fiction.

Leaving time aside, the way we go into flashback can certainly vary. We can do it with dialogue:

"You better not pick that up," I heard Jim say twenty years ago . . .

Or with narrative:

Twenty years I ago I remember Jim telling me not to pick it up, but I wouldn't listen, and we ended up in a big argument. My mother heard us . . .

Or with a different past tense:

I had had an argument with Jim twenty years ago when he told me not to pick it up. I had ignored him and . . .

The point is that flashbacks offer creative opportunity for

storytelling, and because there are varied ways to do it, writers have choices that can add to dramatic effect. Dialogue, for example, would not work with solitary reflection or a character's remembrance of an unaccompanied trek.

But steady narration would work:

Fifteen years before, I stood on this hill, alone, a week's solitary camping behind me, and the pond below had a sheen of crystal light in the center . . .

On the other hand if we wanted to add a bit of characterization, we could write:

"The pond!" I had shouted fifteen years before.
"It's where the map says."
Bob had been amused. "Been here a long, long time, son . . . "

Flashbacks generally provide an anecdotal shift, a new scene with a different setting or a new character or two or perhaps even a variation of the plotline. In film parlance it can highlight "the back story" or give some substance to why things are happening now! But the flashback can also be used for a different purpose, and it may not be an anecdotal shift. See how Saul Bellow does it in his essay, "It All Adds Up."

"Let me turn back four decades to my three-dollar room in the middle of an America where people saw themselves in a collective image as inhabiting down-to-earth, bread-and-butter, meat-and-potatoes, dollars-and-cents, cash-and-carry Chicago . . . "

And he goes on to speak of the general philosophy in Chicago of that day (the 1930s) as overriding materialism. He offers the question of the novelist's place in such a society. He's providing a philosophical/historical image through his flashback, and there's really no anecdotal shift here at all. Yes, he's using time to establish the place-setting, but the rest is a philosophical exploration of a certain way of life, and that's all.

Clearly, then, flashbacks — especially with nonfiction — have more to them than just adding to a story, and just as clearly it may not be necessary to have the platform of a story for a flashback to operate. All that's needed, as Bellow shows us, is a determination to portray a point of view and to tie it to a time sequence — in this case, Chicago in the 1930s. No shift in storyline, no new characterization, no beefed up "back story."

Flashbacks operate best when they are vividly portrayed, when the reader grasps the story development easily. Clarity is important because we want the reader to understand what the flashback offers and how it impacts on the story. The most effective device is one that promotes drama because here we have the reader's attention. And one of the most useful drama-producing effects is contrast . . . a seven-foot man dancing with a five-foot woman . . . a gentle, soft-spoken older man recalling his violent, younger self . . . a professional musician who is tone-deaf. Contrast is what makes these situations attention-grabbing, and it is the drama inherent in them that makes them so.

See how Barry Newman handles it in his portrait of Ernesto Sabrino, now forty years old and formerly a modestly successful matador. He's become a bandillero, one of the "'old men of the bull ring," employed by the matador to soften up the bull prior to the kill. In "Bandillero," Newman quotes a conversation with Sabrino:

"'I always thought I was good,' he says, sitting down
under the bar's television, which is showing a bicycle
race. 'There was one day in Rioja. I had a good bull
that day. I mastered it. I was artistic. I cut two ears.
For me this was success. But I don't build sand castles;
life proved me wrong.'"

This is a very short flashback, more of a nostalgic cut than
anything else. But it serves to demonstrate how use of contrast can bring drama and feeling to a story. Note how he
describes himself that day in Rioja: "I was artistic. I cut two
ears . . . " and then how he deals with what he does today:
". . . I don't build sand castles, life proved me wrong . . . ." In
the one moment he is on top of the world, an artist, a master,
and in the next he is back in the pack, a mediocrity, a realist.
The contrast in his two states of being, especially since they
are adjacent on the page, offers poignant truth about what any
man is capable of becoming: once a champion now an also-
ran, and the drama of the moment drips with sensibility. We
feel his pain, his discomfort and his sadness, yet we come to
accept that it has happened, and we follow the story to its
conclusion.

Contrast, of course, is a form of conflict in that it provides
the seeds for strife and friction. Some contrasts are legendary:
old v. new . . . young v. elderly . . . male v. female . . . rich v.
poor . . . straight v. gay . . . and in each situation the contrast
is inherent in the conflict and in a lot of cases the contrast is
the reason for the conflict. One doesn't need to elaborate on
how these situations often erupt into conflict other than to
state the obvious: where people are different there are bound
to be misconceptions, and these are what lead to drama.

Still another way to give heft to a flashback is by the writer changing point of view so that a different perspective is emphasized. Here's how it works:

> Today's literary agents are not updated versions of those who came before them. Gone are the bonds of personal connection where a writer's *angst* was the agent's general pain; now, it's book contracts signed, copies sold, subsidiary rights offered . . . what a difference! I recall my old agent taking umbrage when an early manuscript of mine was returned by a publisher . . . "Don't worry," she soothed, "we'll sell this; they don't know any better . . . "

The point-of-view shift here is from the objective to the subjective, from third person ("Today's literary agents . . . ") to the first person ("I recall . . . "), and it is the shift to first person that gets us into the flashback. Shifting like this changes the reader's perspective, and in the process it forces the reader to pay close attention because different things seem to be happening. Note that while the writing is in the third person the story proceeds in a rather formal, analytical manner, and there's no hint of what's to come. Then, suddenly, there's a shift, and the writing becomes more personal, more immediate, and the storyline is different.

Garrison Keillor, host of the PBS radio program, *A Prairie Home Companion,* and an accomplished novel- and short-story writer, proves himself adept at using this technique in his essay, "A Return to Basics: Mealtime Without Guilt." The subject is eating, and he says it used to be a joyous activity but no longer, because of " . . . food writers who urge us to cook and eat so-called elegant food instead of substantial food — pick food apart instead of just eat it." Then he flashes back to his youth when he and others were "happy" eaters:

> "Out there in Bruegal, N.D., surrounded by an ocean of durum wheat, we got three squares a day, piled our plates and cried 'Yes!' to seconds. Tables groaned at picnics, church suppers, Sunday dinners, holiday feasts. Food was a relief against our flat landscape . . . "

A page later he reinforces the flashback:

> "When I was a boy way out on the open prairie of the American heartland . . . "

And then, one page after that, he brings us back from the flashback, saying the "great meals" of his youth have been scared off by the food authorities:

> " . . . ridiculed, made to seem cheap and coarse and not in good taste . . . "

Note the switch between points of view — his description of the food writers whose stringent demands on good taste run afoul of the hungry eater whose demands are neither stringent nor always in good taste but who rebels against a buffoon-like character depiction. Keillor is saying the tutti-tutti food writers believe you are what you eat, food's a means to an end, and this is clearly at odds with the wide prairie ethic that says food is an end in itself, a simple, enjoyable undertaking.

The shift of point-of-view isn't really between third and first person, though could make an argument that by quoting the food writers Keillor presents that point of view. Then, in his casual manner, he slips into first person: "Out there in Breugal, N.D., surrounded by an ocean of durum wheat, we . . . " and subtly he gives us the picture of what it was like years ago when folks got together and had a meal. He then reinforces the flashback by becoming more explicit: "When I was a boy way out on the open prairie . . . " and now we have the time set-piece, we know exactly to where and when he was referring us . . . "*When I was a boy . . .* "

What the point of view shift really accomplishes here is to draw a distinction between the tutti-tutti food writers and the down-to-earth eaters of the prairie. And in this distinction we have something already touched upon — contrast. Aren't the food values of the food writers and the heartland eaters in contrast? One reveres "elegant" food, the other worships "steamy mountains of fried chicken." The contrast develops into conflict because the chasm between the two groups is wide and unbreachable. They stare one another down from individual redoubts of certainty, and the reader is intrigued. Who's right, who's wrong isn't the issue so much as what we've learned about attitudes toward food. There is a story here because there's drama in the fact certain food eaters look down their collective noses at certain other food eaters, and that when the attitude is returned, the resentment is palpable.

Food as a subject of conflict is sprinkled through the world of fiction (look no further than *The Caine Mutiny* where Captain Queeg holds a midnight inquisition because a bucket of fresh strawberries had been surreptitiously consumed), but as we see, food as conflict can also be a spark to a work of nonfiction. Nudge the points of view around, provide an appropriate flashback with some contrast and the story comes to life.

As with any other dramatic technique, flashbacks can't be hurled into the story without some reference to the building chronology. Using the food analogy once more, when we create a delicate hollandaise sauce, we don't dump in the lemon without an awareness that if it goes in too early or too late, it will curdle the mixture. Experienced chefs know there is a *right* moment to add the lemon, and only then will the sauce develop well.

So it is with flashbacks. They should be used when the time is right, when a flashback will add to the story and maybe answer some pending questions. Jonathon Penner offers perhaps the best gauge of when that right moment will come: "You won't, in general, insert a flashback right in the middle of fascinating action," he writes. "That merely frustrates the reader, who is trying to find out what happens next — not what happened a long time ago."

As with our hollandaise analogy, you wouldn't add lemon before the budding sauce heats to the point where the lemon can slide in without disrupting the mixture. This would certainly frustrate the diner whose appetite is building in anticipation.

Penner goes on: "But at a certain moment [the reader] will *want* a flashback. He'll want to know how things got like this, what makes these people the way they are . . . ."

And this is the moment when the experienced writer knows it's time to offer a bit of the "back story," to highlight some of the things that haven't come through as clearly up to this point. The art comes in knowing when this moment appears and then applying dramatic effect to enhance the story line.

Flashbacks can, of course, come about at various moments throughout a story, even in the first few pages (though this can be difficult to do unless the initial story line is strong and dramatic in itself, so the flashback won't seem a contrivance to the reader). The point is to understand that when the story *needs* a change of pace or some clarification or a new element, the flashback is there for the taking. In itself it provides dramatic effect by changing the reader's focus from present to past, and it offers the opportunity to expand the existing story line and build on the drama already developed.

The question of when to use flashbacks is as much a concern of nonfiction writers as it is for fiction writers. Nonfiction writers seeking to develop dramatic effect for their work see flashbacks as integral for their stories, and they use them accordingly. Look no further than John McPhee whose nonfiction works have covered a multitude of subjects in a multitude of geographic areas. Critics have hailed his use of fiction-writing devices such as deep characterization, dialogue and scene setting while complimenting him on his factual presentations. His work rises to the level of art even if it is not fiction.

Here he is in an early book, *Pieces of the Frame,* traveling the highways of Georgia with a couple of scientists. They are looking for "roadkill" (what he calls "D. O. R." for "dead on road"), anything that had been alive until it met death on the highway. The purpose? To analyze migratory habits of whatever they came upon. In the first few pages McPhee describes the group finding a mortally wounded snapping turtle and he describes how it dies and how the scientists preserve it in the field for future examination. Eighteen pages later he finally lets us in on why he is with the scientists:

"Sam had been a friend of mine for some years, and when he wrote to say that he was now travelling around the state collecting skulls and pelts, eating rattlesnakes, preserving natural areas, and charting the range of river frogs, I could not wait to go down and see . . . "

But this really isn't a true flashback. It may serve the same purpose (explanation and story development, drama and characterization), but it doesn't give us the requisite *time* element; we don't know when Sam wrote and how long they had been travelling around the state together. It doesn't give us a completely new scene.

Two pages later, however, McPhee sets it right. We're now twenty pages into the book, and at this point we're wondering how the author reacted when he first hit the road with the scientists. After all, looking for "roadkill" isn't something a lot of us are prepared for. McPhee clearly had no problem with it, and he describes his first sally on the Georgia roads:

"The D.O.R.'s that first day included a fan belt Sam took for a blacksnake — jammed on his brakes, backed up to see — and a banana peel that Carol identified at first glimpse as a jumping mouse. Eager was the word for them. They were so much on the hunt . . . "

Note that McPhee follows what Jonathon Penner suggests: insert the flashback when it's appropriate to do so and not before. Here he is twenty pages into the book, and he finally tells us how it was on the first day McPhee accompanied the scientists. The important thing to recognize is that chronology plays a secondary role to story line here, and for the author it was more important to establish the drama in the story (searching for dead animals along the road) than to explain either why he was there or how he fared on the first day. But McPhee also recognized that these were questions we, the readers, will want to understand at some point, and he provides the answers to us *after* he has set the dramatic scene of the three searching and finding the mortally wounded turtle. Once he establishes what the author and the others are doing on these roads, then he can turn his attention to filling in the blanks of our curiosity.

In the meantime the flashback works the way it should work, providing heft to the story line, giving the overall drama a push.

And showing us how an accomplished nonfiction writer produces a work of art.

8.

Inter-cut Those Scenes!

Ever witnessed a fashion photo-shoot? The model adjusts her (or his) pose, nods as final instructions are given, takes a deep breath and holds it . . . and holds it . . .

The photographer aims, his words flowing:
"Nice! Good!"
Click!
Click! Click!
"Great!"
Click! Click! Click!
"Head! Remember the head!"
Click!

You stand quietly on the side. The exercise is, after all, a rather simple act, one model, one photographer, one camera — it could be a recipe for boredom. There's hardly movement, and any writer knows that lack of movement in an unfolding scene spells disaster.

We have a word for it: stasis, something stationary,

116

unmoving. Boredom personified.

But then you're aware of something else. A tiny nudge of excitement, a feeling of interest, you stare at the model, stare at the photographer . . . there's unfolding art here, the creation of . . . something!

And you realize the energy from that creation is what has you, back and forth, photographer, model . . . model, photographer . . . a scene, two scenes developing, and the excitement is in the quick moves, the back and forth . . .

It is the feeling of excitement that writers strive to develop because readers will stay glued to the page, and there isn't a writer alive who doesn't want *that* to happen! If a static scene like the photographer and the model can generate excitement, then we ought to be able to take the written word and make it perform effortlessly. Using words to create excitement is the sort of thing writers must be able to do, and the form of the story shouldn't matter.

In fiction, for example, we can portray the photographer and the model as former lovers who develop sexual heat each time they work together. The accomplished fiction writer doesn't need to use many words to portray it.

With nonfiction the only difference is that we have to stay with the facts, and if the facts are that the photographer and model were former lovers, then the story line will mirror the fiction writer's story line with the same results. The nonfiction writer can show sexual heat from the words exchanged or from the body language or from what is not said so long as it actually happened!

The excitement derived from wordplay is an underpin of drama in the story, and it is how we employ the wordplay that will determine the level of excitement (and hence, drama), whom it will envelop and how it plays out. For example, with our photographer and model, suppose the photographer has a secret crush on the model but never divulged it, wouldn't the wordplay be more subtle, less demonstrative than if both had feelings for the other?

Or if neither had interest in the other, could there still be emotional involvement? What if one sees a meal ticket, as someone who could open various career doors, or alternatively as an impediment to a career? In any of these cases, the level of emotion rises as the mutual involvement rises.

It is just this that brings us to a useful technique using wordplay and page graphics to create and present dramatic nonfiction.

I'm referring to scene intercuts, the ability to change scenes rapidly enough so the very act of change generates excitement . . . and hence, drama. Think back to the photographer and the model and the quick attention-changes we experienced. If we lingered too long on one or the other, the excitement would die quickly because we weren't shifting our focus fast enough, and if we stayed focused on either of them too long, we'd soon grow bored because neither was generating much action.

But by going back and forth (as in a tennis match), we make the sense of excitement build . . .

And that's exactly what rapid scene inter-cutting does! Katherine Ramsland spoke of it in *The Writer's Handbook* in 1991. She was referring to short chapters (but aren't they really just separate scenes?) which she said " . . . can give the feeling of tension, impatience and urgency . . . ." Short chapters, one following the next, rat-a-tat-tat . . . no time to get settled and grow langorous, change, change, change . . .

This is what we mean by scene intercuts, quick changes, not allowing the reader to get settled. It is wordplay and page graphics rolled together, it's what we read and what we see on the page, and the combination flies into our conscious awareness and produces a sense of excitement because things are happening fast!

Take Gerald Clarke's biography of Truman Capote, titled simply *Capote*. Almost every scene is no more than two or three pages, and as we read we get the sense of movement, of quick "takes" because this seems to be the way Capote lived his life, never in one place very long.

In the early 1970s Capote joined the rock group, Rolling Stones, on a thirty-one-city tour. He intended to do a story on them, but after spending a few days with the group, he decided not to follow through. The scene, which runs about two pages, ends:

> "Later in an interview with the magazine [*Rolling Stone*], he admitted that if he had been twenty-five years younger — and if he had not already written a history of a musical tour — he just might have been bothered. But why, he asked 'should I do a game that I've done?'"

The next scene, which runs only a page, begins:

> "It was a good question, but it didn't stop him from engaging in other games he had already done . . . "

This scene ends with a new friend, Bob MacBride, bemoaning the end of his relationship with Capote. MacBride writes in his diary:

> "'Dreamed that Capote returned.' But that Truman did not do."

The next scene goes on for a bit more than a page and begins:

> "The explanation was simple: Truman was in
> love again . . . "

The quick scene cuts give an oomph to the drama because everything is happening quickly. But the author wants to focus on Capote's whimsical ways, and the sudden changes in course he seemed to follow. How better than to shorten the scenes and ratchet up the pace? The reader gets caught up in the movement and feels the building drama.

And we actually get two separate benefits: we gain a rush of excitement because the writer doesn't let us settle in before the scene changes, and we also gain a close insight into the character of Truman Capote. We learn more about him by virtue of the pace of the writing. It's similiar to appreciating the driveability of an outstanding automobile by pushing it to its top speed; the faster it goes, the more it hugs the road and offers comfort, and the more we understand why it carries a high price tag!

Writing pace, in other words, can be a metaphor for characterization, though it's not wise to push it too far because pace, is, after all, only a writing *technique*, not a substantive conclusion. We rely on pace to provide us one path to understand, perhaps, a single character, as well as to expand dramatic opportunities. But pace can't do it alone. It is not central enough for that. Pace is a tool that can be stirred up by inter-cutting short scenes. It is not the essence of the story line.

The use of scene intercuts, however, does work well when we seek to dramatize our nonfiction, and in this sense it's no different from what fiction writers do. Look at some of the work of Ed McBain, the author of many police procedurals, for example. Sometimes he'll have two- or three-line scenes, just a snippet of the action or a single back-and-forth of dialogue, and then it's on to the next scene. When he does this, it's clear he wants to maintain a high level of suspense or excitement, and the success he's had with his works attests to his ability to achieve what he seeks.

There's no reason why nonfiction writers can't use the same approach and with the same results. But even with the shortest scene, we have to be aware that excitement or drama is what we're after. We can't lose that perspective while we concentrate on creating short scenes. In other words, the size of the scenes we wish to inter-cut is not the key; the end product — drama — is what we're after, and the short scenes should contribute to that. If our short scene intercuts don't seem to generate greater excitement than what we had before, we should probably do away with them and try some other technique to bolster our drama.

But in every scene, long or short, where we want drama build-up, there's a key sentence or phrase that opens the door for us. Outdoor writer John Barsness, who specializes in adventure and nature writing, puts it simply and clearly: "If possible, concentrate on one key sentence to set the scene, rather than a paragraph," he writes. "Set the scene as quickly as possible. Then get on with the action."

One key sentence . . . it can take any form. Suppose we're writing about bird-watching along the John Muir Trail in California, and we come upon a bird-of-prey nest on a high outcropping. An adult bird has come with a live catch in its talons. We must set the scene quickly, and we can do it with sharp description:

It will be a quick death, the rapier beak and knife-like claws ripping the prey apart . . .

Or we can do it with dialogue:

"Look, the little ones are watching like it's some kind of ceremony . . ."

Or we can do it with a question:

How many of us ponder, really think about, the cruelties in nature, the agonizing, hard realities? . . .

Or we can do it with an imperative:

We will watch what will follow, and we will do it without slumping into unwarranted sympathies . . .

Note the common thread with each of these choices: the sentence sets the scene, and the action comes after. The key sentence acts as a platform for the action so that the details can build on what has been set up.

The important thing for us is to recognize how this fits with our attempts to use quick scene intercuts. We must focus on that key sentence as we develop each scene, even if we plan to run the scene only a few lines. Obviously if the scene consists of one sentence, then that becomes the key one; but if we have two or more sentences in our scene, we must be sure to open with a sentence that sets the tone for what will follow.

For example, if we take the scene of the bird of prey with its quarry, we wouldn't open the scene with poetic description of the horizon, sky and cloud colors because they are not key to the essence of our scene: the dispatching of quarry by a bird of prey and subsequent feeding of its young. We'd start by showing the bird of prey in action, arriving at the nest to begin the feeding process.

Take a look at the way Miles Corwin uses key sentences to set scenes in his book, *The Killing Season*, a story of homicide detectives in Los Angeles, California, during a recent spring. Note the opening sentences in four succeeding scenes:

[page 25] "Homicide detectives in South-Central Los Angeles usually do not wait long for for murder. On Detective Marcella Winn's first weekend on call, she spends an edgy Friday evening at home . . ."

[page 26] "On this cool, breezy spring weekend, Felipe Angeles Gonzales spends Friday night at home, a small South-Central bungalow that he shares with nine other recent immigrants from Mexico City . . ."

[page 27] "It seems to Winn that she just closed her eyes when the telephone finally rings . . ."

[page 28] "Winn meets Detective Pete 'Raz' Razankas, who is waiting at a police station parking lot in an unmarked squad car, engine running . . ."

None of these scenes runs longer than a page, and each one revs the action and builds the drama. The third scene ("It seems to Winn . . ."), in fact, runs only ten lines, but note in each case how the opening sentence develops the action to follow: homicide detectives "usually do not wait . . . ," Gonzales

"spends Friday night at home . . . ," Winn "just closed her eyes
. . . ," Winn "meets Dectective Pete . . ." Then the scene proceeds to develop what the opening sentence has set out.

And in each case it's done within a page or less.

Corwin touches on another technique as well: his use of
time and date at the opening of each scene so the reader gets a
good handle on the rapidity with which things are developing:

"At four o'clock, the door swung open . . ."
"Sixteen minutes later, the wedding cake was wheeled
into the room . . .
"At 6:04 the telephone rang as planned . . ."

Each of these is a device for scene setting, and when they
are used to open a series of short scenes, the sense of excitement, suspense, uncertainty, etc., has to build. Corwin doesn't
employ the device completely, but he does rely on it to an extent:

"On this cool, breezy spring weekend . . ."
"It seems to Winn that she just closed her eyes . . ."

Time, then, was definitely on Corwin's mind as he set out
his four scenes, and time became the crank that revved up his
drama.

Take a look at a more elaborate use of *time and date* in
the early portion of John Dinges and Saul Landau's book,
Assassination on Embassy Row, the story of the killing of a
Chilean diplomat, Orlando Letellier, and his American secre-
tary in Washington, D.C., in the 1970s. The authors set the
scene of the assassination with short takes — seventeen separate scenes in the first twenty-two pages of the book, and
they frequently open with time:

[page 3] "September 9, 1976. At Kennedy International Airport the arrival of . . ."

[page 14] "September 11-14. Townley didn't waste time thinking . . ."

[page 16] "Midnight, September 15, 1976. Virgilio Paz and Townley drove in Paz's rust-colored Volvo . . ."

[page 17] "September 17, 1976. Letellier drove from his Bethesda home . . ."

[page 17] "September 18, 1976. Jose Dionisio Suarez drove to Washington . . ."

[page 23] "September 20, 1976. Townley set out to do chores in Miami . . ."

By use of time and date the authors give us a running account of what the characters are doing at any particular time, and since the scenes shift back and forth between Letellier and the band of assassins, we understand that with each time-step, the two worlds are coming closer, closer . . . and eventually they will collide. The reader certainly appreciates the clarity the time-steps offer because there's no uncertainty when something important happens. *Time and date* give us a picture already framed. What's left for the author is to color it in and mark the portrayals sharply and distinctly.

And when this is done, and the scenes are short and snappy, we'll reach that level of excitement that keeps the reader glued to the page.

In a real sense what we're discussing here is a literary device known as a "transition," a word or phrase that eases our jump from scene to scene or place to place within a scene. Most of us have used some form of transition throughout our lives in letters or post cards or diary entries or school papers, and there's nothing inherently difficult about them. For example, we're writing to a friend and describing some recent event. Our focus then changes, and we write, "In the meantime . . ." or "Yesterday I had a . . ." or "Mom is coming to town next week . . ."

What the transition does is to offer a smooth way to ease out of one scene and into another, and there are many, many transitions available for use. When applied to scene inter-cutting the use of quick time-dates piled on top of one another, as we see above, makes it quite easy to shift focus and keep the drama. But there are other ways of accomplishing this, as well. Blanche Kirchner gives us some in a recent article:

> "As a writer, you may have to skip over time periods,
> bounce between locations, present contrasting ideas,
> and still make sense if you use suitable transitions . . ."

She offers what she calls "bridging" words and phrases: *yet, however, furthermore* . . . then she calls up more general words and phrases: *besides, granted that, speaking of, in addition* . . . Each of these accomplishes the purpose of shifting focus, even if slightly, and this keeps the drama level from collapsing.

The point is transitions are what we use to shift, change or inter-cut scenes, and sometimes they can get quite elaborate. Take, for example, this piece by Bill Barich, "Magic," which was part of a 1980 volume of his personal essays on horses and horse racing, *Laughing in the Hills.* The selection runs only seventeen pages, and it contains ten scenes, so each scene averages less than two pages. It's the story of his stay in a motel near a California racetrack and his study of why people love horse racing, handicapping and betting. The very nature of gambling, of course, provides dramatic ingredients, so we don't need to look very far to find an interesting story line. The questions are fairly universal:

— will he win money or won't he?
— what unusual characters does he encounter, and how do they affect him?
— were there any exciting races? Does he describe them?
— does he observe any one winning or losing large sums?

But the story itself, since it is *his* story, may not contain all the excitement the reader seeks (because, after all, he's *studying* the bettor, and some readers will find that a turn-off). So Barich injects some creative juice into his scene intercuts, and now we have a rather unusual mix of transitions that follow not only time and date but point of view, too. See how it works in these adjoining scenes:

[page 325] "I sat by the Terrace [motel where he's staying] swimming pool, reading about magic . . ."
[page 326] "In 1460 a Macedonian monk brought Cosimo de' Medici a manuscript reputed to be an incomplete copy of the secret magical *Corpus Hermeticum* . . ."
[page 329] "The race was for two-year olds, a five furlong spring, and I looked over the stock in the paddock . . ."
[page 331] "All week long I kept winning . . ."

Two scenes later he picks up the story of magic in the ancient world, describing how Pico, a 15th century Venetian writer who had written about magic, intended to kidnap his mistress from her Medici husband: "When Pico fell in love, he did so with abandon . . . ."

Barich is using a couple of different inter-cut techniques,

and he's interspersing them through the article: note how he develops *time-date* inter-cutting:

"In 1460 . . ."
"All week long . . ."

Then note how he changes point of view from scene to scene:

"I sat by the Terrace . . ."
"In 1460 . . ."
"The race was . . . and I looked over . . ."

The *time-date* inter-cutting not only begins each scene with a specific time-date reference, but there is a contrast between present and past: Barich moves easily between his days at the track and the historical references to magic (as well as to other historical items not included here). Present and past give nice symmtery to any storyline, especially if the changes move back and forth quickly and easily. The inter-cutting keeps things moving, and the reader keeps a high level of awareness.

But he also changes scenes through use of different points of view. He switches back and forth between first person ("I sat by the Terrace . . .") and third person ("In 1460 . . ."). Each time he changes the point of view (and there are times when his scenes run a half-page, so the point-of-view shifts can be quick), and redirects the reader's focus, we've noted it's that change of focus for the reader that can generate action and excitement. A note of caution, though: shifting the point of view simply to create scene intercuts is dangerous because we run the risk of the procedural tail wagging the substantive dog

— that is, do the scene inter-cuts affect the pace, quality and overall pattern of our story? Is the reader confused by the myriad shifts? If so, then we need to slow them down.

But the basic point remains: we can use point of view shifting to bolster our scene inter-cutting, and as we see with Bill Barich, a judicious use of the technique will add to the excitement and force of the work. Scene inter-cutting works, it builds drama because it tends to speed things along, not allowing bog-down or stasis in the storyline.

Click! goes the camera.

Click, click!

"Hold it! says the photographer.

"Like this?" asks the model . . .

Click! . . . click! . . .

"Beautiful . . ."

9.

Tingle Those Senses!

When live, hour-long television drama was a staple for millions of American households, one show offered something no other competing show could match. It had to do with, of all things, the commercials aired around the show. The sponsor was a well-known food company, and dishes using company products, particularly cheeses and sauces, were dramatically prepared and displayed on camera. The moist, velvety voice of Ed Herlihy described . . . soft, delicate mixtures glistening with freshness, heated to a tingle, served in creamy, rich texture, giving off syrupy aroma . . .

Any television viewer unmoved by the presentation had to be wearing ear phones and blinders! There was no way to avoid salivating . . . and, of course, the food sponsor was well aware of it: appeal to the viewers' senses, and they'll go out and buy the products; show them delicious taste, and the image will remain! People remember what they feel, especially if the feelings are vividly induced. A strong sense of taste, an eye-opening food serving, anything that brings up the appetite level, and the pleasure principle emerges . . . and it demands satisfaction!

People *want* to enjoy what they eat. Imagine the food company advertising/marketing people brainstorming:

"Get them thinking about . . . us!"
"Paint a picture?"
"Right, so it sticks."
"Image, my friends . . . "
"A cheese sauce is image?"
"It'll sure make it taste better!"

And that's the point, of course. If the commercial could plant an appealing image in the viewer's head, then when that viewer comes face to face with the product, the inclination to enjoy it will be there waiting . . . even before it's consumed.

Call it a bias, perhaps, but the viewer has been conditioned to like the company's products because of the presentation. There's been an appeal to the viewer's senses, to the mental imagery and impressions we all carry with us, and we're conditioned to like what will be put before us because of what we've seen and what we've been told.

Note the dramatic effect. Creating that mental image of an appetizing dish is the key, and once the viewer has that, he or she is definitely part of — inside of, really — what's unfolding on the screen.

Is it any different with the written word? Unlike the television camera which can display three-dimensional images, we writers have only the blank page and our ability to put words on them with power and drama. But we succeed because readers are willing to be patient while we labor to develop a story line that will consume them. It's not instant imagery in the way it is with television, but the effect — creation of a mind picture, an impression — is the same. We both strive to induce the viewer/reader to embrace our story, even if it's a television commercial, because once it happens, dramatic success is assured.

Art and artistry flow from this; it's what moves reader, or viewer, and as we know, one of the classic pillars of art is its effect. What one takes away from exposure to art is the real issue, and if we're unmoved by a work of art, we should not always blame ourselves. Think of it this way: are we *incapable* of gaining something from a work of art? Or, perhaps, is it some failing in the artist who wasn't skillful enough to reach us?

Questions like this are at the root of dramatic writing — nonfiction as well as fiction — because it is in the drama that the threads of artistry appear. Can there be artistry without drama? It would be hard to visualize Michelangelo's Sistine Chapel without feeling the beauty, the color, the imagery, the dramatic effects . . . or to take in the arresting imperatives in Tchaikovsky's *1812 Overture* without sensing the mighty life-and-death clash he portrayed . . . or to empathize with criminals and victims in Truman Capote's *In Cold Blood* but for the multi-layered arresting characterizations he developed. In each instance the artist appeals to something inside us, some sensibility, that allows us to *feel*!

For writers most of that comes down to the senses: touching, hearing, seeing, tasting, smelling. It's here we sow our dramatic oats with the reader, and it's here our artistry can flower. Writers who can draw their readers' senses into the story have a willing audience for whatever comes. For example, suppose we write:

> Hardy watched the small boat miss the
> dock again . . . for the third time, and he

wondered what they were thinking . . .

Is there an appeal to the senses in here? Beyond watching and thinking is Hardy doing any feeling, smelling hearing etc?
Suppose, instead, we write it this way:

Hardy shuddered as the biting wind swirled
around him, its whine steady, ominous.
God, that little boat missed the dock again, he
could taste the fear they must be feeling . . .

Note the senses we've brought up: touch (Hardy "shuddered" . . .), hearing (whine "steady" . . .), taste ("fear" . . .). Doesn't this make for more interesting writing? Don't we feel part of the scene?

That's the value of sense appeal: it generates drama and the artistry that goes with it. As we "appeal" to the senses of the reader, we find the reader responding because we've heightened the drama by including the reader in the story. Once the reader "feels," the connection between reader and story is made, and we have a ready audience for wherever we want our story to go.

Obviously, this type of approach works well with fiction. Take a look at this excerpt from Thomas Mann's *Confessions of Felix Krull, Confidence Man* where a roomful of food is described:

" . . . There were rows and rows of hams
and sausages of all shapes and colors —
white, yellow, red and black; fat and lean
and round and long — rows of canned
preserves, cocoa and tea, bright translucent-

glass bottles of honey, marmalade and jam . . ."

Think back to the opening of this chapter and the description of the television commercial that played on our senses of taste and sight, and here we have the same thing, only this time it's solely with the written word. The appeal is clearly to taste and sight because we're asked to visualize what all of this looks like, but implied, as well, is an appeal to our sense of smell because these sausages probably give off an odor . . . all of this in a short fiction paragraph.

The same type of approach can be used with nonfiction. After all, Mann simply describes a room filled with food, and that type of scene is easily duplicated in real life. For us, the important thing isn't that we can find such a room, but . . . how . . . do . . . we . . . describe . . . it! Note Mann uses strong adjectives ("fat," "lean," "round," "bright"), he also interjects colors ("red," "black . . . ") and he describes the foods specifically ("hams," "sausages," "marmalade," "cocoa" . . .). All of this to get an image into our minds, and does he succeed?

Absolutely, and if it can be done with fiction, it can be done with nonfiction. Sally-Jo Bowman says, "Use as many of the senses as you can," and she advises to "engage" the reader's senses by means of description and setting a scene. Think "irresistibly delicious nonfiction," she encourages, and the story should take care of itself.

Another way of looking at it is to think of the physical reactions events or people may create in a story. For example, we witness a child struck by an auto; we could write it factually:

> "At one minute after ten this morning, a six-year old boy ran into the street chasing a ball and a car driven by a neighborhood man couldn't swerve in time . . . "

Or we could write it:

"John Vinson had a vision of what was going to
happen moments before it occurred: the laughing
six year old would ignore his mother and run
into the rainy, slippery street after the green and
white ball his absent father had mailed . . . "

Which offers more reader identification? Obviously the
second description because we can *feel* what John Vinson
feels and see what he sees. In the first description it's an
objective, uninvolved narrator giving us the information, and
while the facts may be the same in both cases, one moves us
and places us *inside* the scene while the other keeps us fenced
outside, observing.

This is the way writing that appeals to the senses is sup-
posed to work — it provides a dramatic basis for story movement. And appealing to the senses is just as appropriate with
nonfiction as it is with fiction. Here's what Hayes Jacobs, a
former editor with *Writer's Digest Magazine,* has to say: "Nonfiction focuses on facts, but to impress the reader with facts,
one must be aware of his emotions — how he *feels* about
things, as well as what he thinks of them . . . ."

Note what he emphasizes: how the reader "feels" about
what he or she reads. This, to Jacobs, is as important as providing the reader with information so he or she can "think"
about what is written. Feeling and thinking . . . basically two
sides of the same coin. which is reader-involvement. And
since we're concerned with "dramatic" nonfiction writing,
there certainly is a place for anything that seeks to reach the
reader's feelings.

Take a look at *The Kiss,* Kathryn Harrison's memoir of an

incestuous affair with her father. She takes up with him at age twenty after he'd been absent for many years, and she is caught in a vise of shame and guilt and longing. She describes him when they are parting at the airport after he'd re-entered her life and spent a week at her mother's house. At this point the incest had not occurred:

> "My father looks at me, then, as no one
> has ever looked at me before. His hot eyes
> consume me — eyes that I will discover are
> always this bloodshot. I almost feel their
> touch. He takes my hands, one in each of
> his, and turns them over, stares at my
> palms. He does not actually kiss them,
> but his look is one that ravishes . . . "

What senses does Harrison appeal to here? The sense of touch certainly; note how she puts it: "His hot eyes *consume* me . . . " and that is clearly a physical reaction. In fact she underscores it by writing that she could almost feel the "touch" of his eyes. And a sentence or so later she speaks of his stare at her hands as if he was to "ravish" them — again a physical reaction and one that flows from touch.

But note what also is here: there's an appeal to the sense of sight, to what is *seen*! Harrison refers to what she sees as her father focuses his look on her face and then on her hands. No one, she says, has ever looked at her like that, and she underscores it when she characterizes his stare at her hands as one of ravishment! It's clearly a powerful moment in the book, and the way she describes her father's stares has to unsettle even the stoniest reader. What she sees is both threatening ("look is one that ravishes . . . ") and surrendering

("His hot eyes consume me . . . "), and as we read these words we can feel her emotions. It's exactly what Hayes Jacobs suggests: as we write we should remain aware of the reader's *feelings*, and in this instance, Kathryn Harrison has done just that. She provides us with a scene where powerful emotions are at work, and she encourages us to feel these emotions along with her.

Dramatic touches are what help to build this scene. For example, she uses the occasional strong adjective: bloodshot eyes, "hot" eyes, ravishing looks, and this ratchets up the emotional content. But we, too, can use these strong adjectives when our purpose is to build sense appeal. For example, which of the following sweeps up our attention more forcibly:

> She had a pretty mouth, and she used
> such nice words . . .
> Her mouth glistened with erotic promise,
> her syrupy words flowed into my heart . . .

Clearly, the second sentence would capture our attention more readily because it conjures an image and appeals to our senses and emotions. We use "strong" adjectives to achieve this, active, image-creating adjectives that provide dramatic content. Think, for example, of each of the senses and a strong adjective that might go with them:

sight . . . . *flash*
hearing . . . *roar*
touch . . . . .. *rip*
smell . . . . .. *suffocate*
taste . . . . .. *choke*

Then apply these, or similar, adjectives to the description we're writing, and — bingo! — we have sense appeal because we've made a strong enough pitch to the reader's emotions. Each of these strong adjectives conjures an image in the reader's mind, and after all, that's what we're really after.

There's another device Kathryn Harrison uses to build sense appeal, and that's to "personalize" a part of the body offering senses, to turn it into metaphor: normally, the hands "touch," the eyes "see," the mouth "tastes" and so forth. Note what she has done to a single body part in this description: the hot eyes "consume," they don't just see; she has given them action, she has given them life. Then the eyes almost "touch" her, they go beyond seeing, and once more she has given them life; his look "ravishes," it doesn't just mark her, and here again the senses *act* in the strongest possible manner.

By doing this she gives the reader a chance to feel the personalizing effect of the eyes that "consume" or the look that "ravishes," and the readers' impressions are bound to be swayed. It isn't simply a disembodied "look" or a pair of nondescript eyes, it's a look with fired purpose and eyes that breathe. Everything in the scene is now alive metaphorically, and the drama flows.

Personalizing a body part to establish sense appeal is something all nonfiction writers should be able to do. Take our mouths . . . if we want to personalize them, how about:

His crooked smile brought a knot of fear
to my belly . . .

or

Her thick lips devoured my slight
indecision . . .

Try it with the nose where the sense of smell operates:

He smelled the five wooded miles
she had struggled through . . .

or

Her nose darted in a frantic search for some
lingering odor . . .

The point is this: when we "personalize" a body part, give it a metaphorical lift and provide it some strong action, an appeal to the reader's senses will surely follow. All we need do is to decide what sense or senses we should appeal to and how thorough that appeal should be.

Thoroughness . . . it's a key question when we seek to develop sense appeal. How much, how little do we need to add so the reader becomes engaged? If we do too much, the reader will grow desensitized and the effects will be lost; too little, and the effect may never get off the ground. But if there is a general rule, it's better to add more than less because good sense appeal is based upon details, and a lasting impression is only made when enough details make the image vivid enough. It is in these details that the essence of sense appeal can be found, and Rita Berman in her piece, "Creative Nonfiction Writing," speaks to it directly:

"Specific details are highly significant in nonfiction
articles to help the reader visualize the place or
event you are describing. They add interest and
color and convey atmosphere and mood to the
setting, locale, time of year and even the weather . . . "

It's the image we hope to place in the reader's mind that we seek to develop, and a series of details will certainly accomplish that. Compare these two sentences:

They walked outside and looked at the
evening sky, a few stars, the moon,
some faint clouds, that's all there was.

Outside, the white moon glowed, the stars
hovered overhead, the air shimmered with
velvet music, the faraway clouds buffered
the night sky and the scent of jasmine floated.

There's a difference of course, and the difference is in the details. In the first selection there are sky, moon, stars and clouds but presented without any attempt at sense appeal. It's merely a laundry list of what could be seen. But in the second selection we add a couple of details — the air and the scent of jasmine . . . and we make a concerted effort at sense appeal by some personalizing of inanimate objects — moon "glowed," stars "hovered," air "shimmered," scent "floated," and the result is a much more satisfying description. Rita Berman is right as far as she goes: details do help the reader to visualize . . . what's also needed is to take those details and apply sense-appeal adjectives and/or verbs, and then the image for the reader will really stand out.

One of the most vivid nonfiction works of the past sixty years was John Hersey's story about the atom bombing of the Japanese city, Hiroshima, in August, 1945. In his book Hersey portrays the devastation and the chaos that inevitably followed the dropping of the bomb, and while the scenes themselves don't need much dressing up because of their innate vividness, it's in the details that we get a true sense of what went on. Without these details, the horror and the panic wouldn't be quite so overwhelming. But Hersey gives us the story simply and cleanly and memorably; here he describes a moment in Asano Park a few hours after the blast where some of the victims had fled. It had begun to rain, and for a bit of time the victims thought the Americans were dropping gasoline from the sky to burn the survivors; then as the rain fell the wind grew stronger:

> " . . . and suddenly — probably because
> of the tremendous convection set up by
> the blazing city — a whirlwind ripped through
> the park. Huge trees crashed down . . . a wild
> array of flat things revolved into a twisting
> funnel — pieces of iron, roofing, papers, doors,
> strips of matting . . . "

Note the array of details here: items of nature ("Huge trees crashed down . . . ") and man-made objects (" . . . a twisting funnel . . . "). He uses strong adjectives: *tremendous* convection . . . , *blazing* city . . . , *Huge* trees . . . , *wild* array . . . . He also includes staunch, action-oriented verbs: whirlwind *ripped* . . . , trees *crashed* . . . , small ones *uprooted and flew* . . . , flat things *revolved* . . .

All of this has a single purpose: to plant an image in the reader's mind, and to make it vivid enough that there will be no forgetting. His sense appeal isn't metaphorical in that he doesn't try to personalize body parts or transform something inanimate into a living, breathing organism. What he does is to paint a careful, clear picture of exactly what happened, offering sufficient details so the reader has no doubt, and then he allows these details to plant the image in the reader's mind. The details, themselves, do the job here because the scene is vivid enough without any additional brush strokes. Our senses are affected by the author's controlled recitation of the facts, and in certain cases, such as this, that is enough.

But *Hiroshima* is hardly a normal book about a normal situation, and while Hersey's approach is instructive, his subject matter was special and we should recognize it as such. Nevertheless, when the details of an event are excruciatingly vivid — as they were for John Hersey — a direct appeal to the senses with its resulting dramatic effects can work with a simple recitation of the facts.

Usually, though, we have to give the facts a boost, and that means reaching out for the reader's senses. Make the facts sing . . . don't make them mumble!

10.

Shift That Point of View!

I recall my law school professor in the course on Evidence. He set up a scenario in the opening moments of class which tested our powers of observation and the limits on our point of view.

One student grabbed a book from another student and ran from the classroom. A few seconds earlier the student whose book was taken had quietly pilfered his next-desk neighbor's pen. *That* student wasn't aware of it because he had gathered *his* next-desk neighbor's attention and pointed out the window to construction being set up outside the building . . . this series of chain events went through half a dozen students, all set up by the professor ahead of time, no student aware that he or she was anything but the main cog in a tiny scenario.

When the student ran from the room, there was surprise and puzzled laughter; the professor waited for things to quiet down, then he asked the person sitting next to the one who had fled the room:

"What did you see?"

She said she had seen the book-pilfering and the escape.

The professor turned to the student who had been pointing out the window. "What did you see?"

"A construction crane and workers getting ready to do some work," was the reply.

"You didn't see anyone steal a book?"

The student admitted he hadn't. Then the professor asked the person whose book had been taken what he had seen, and the answer was he had seen his book stolen and the thief make an escape.

Had he looked out the window at the construction crew? No, he hadn't because he had been too busy.

"Doing what?" the professor wanted to know.

"Stealing his" . . . pointing . . . "pen."

The professor turned to the class. "Anyone else see that pen stolen?" One hand shot up about three rows away. "I did, he was real sneaky."

"Did you also see that construction crew outside?" No, the student admitted he hadn't.

"Did you see the book being stolen?"

No, again.

"Only the pen being taken?"

A nod.

The professor pointed at the student who had watched the construction outside, "if all of you were Mr. ____, would you believe there are thieves in this room?"

A loud "Yes!" resounded. The professor reminded the students that Mr. ____ had not seen any thievery, and the class was going on what others had said. "It's the point of view that controls here," he said, "it's the question of through whose 'means of perception' we're getting our information and our story. If it's the person who sees the thing happen, that's about as reliable as it gets."

Then the professor drew a distinction with information that comes second-hand or in the "he-said-that-she-said-that-he-said . . . " manner. "If the point of view is muddled and uncertain, there's no way of testing the reliability of the information and so we give it very little credence." He turned back to his class-opening scenario: "Those who saw the thievery — pen and/or book — have a clear point of view about what you saw, and you can speak factually about it. By the same token you *didn't* see what was out the window, so whatever you say was out there has to come from someone else's perception. Hence your point of view — your credibility — is clouded on that issue."

The professor could have been talking to a group of writers instead of law students because the demands of point of view are equally strict. We tell our stories from a point of view, we write from a point of view, we seek to immerse readers in our point of view. But the point of view must contain sufficient connection to the ultimate story so the reader won't feel slighted; that is, the reader must feel comfortable going through the story in the skin of the character whose point of view is being used. For example, with a story of murder and intrigue on a private estate, would the gardener's point of view make good reading if he or she was never involved in any of the events, reported only hearsay facts and had no impact on the storyline?

Of course not. But what if the gardener did hear something or was told something by one of the principles or had a series of unsavory experiences with one or more of the characters? This ratchets up the importance of the gardener's point of view, and gives spice and drama to the story.

The crucial thing to understand about point of view, in nonfiction as well as fiction, is that it is one character's "means of perception" about what is happening on the page.

Ultimately, it may be challenged (take a look at the storm engendered by Joe McGinnis in his *Fatal Vision* where his relating of the story surrounding Dr. Jeffrey MacDonald's conviction for murdering his wife and children landed him in a libel action which he finally settled), but the point of view belongs to the actor, and this is the conduit through which the reader absorbs what happens.

There are several point-of-view categories that writers use, and each of them has a specific purpose. Any experienced writer plans his or her point of view carefully ahead of time, testing the proposed storyline to see which would be most effective. There is *first person subjective* where the actor is the "I" of the story. That is, the narrator, the one telling the story, is doing it from his or her perspective, and all the events are developed that way.

> "The next day I decided to get in touch
> with one of the witnesses . . . "

Here, the narrator has placed himself/herself in the middle of the story and is a part of it. Everything is seen or done through the eyes of the first-person narrator, and in that lie both the benefits and limitations of the device. Benefits because the reader will feel closer to the story when the character's personal, subjective viewpoint is presented. When we hear or read, "I feel" . . . or "I think" . . . doesn't it seem more immediate, more *right there*! than if it had been "He feels" . . . or "He thinks . . . ?"

The limits on this device, however, shouldn't be overlooked. By virtue of keeping everything personal, the narrator can only develop a storyline within the confines of his or her world (memoir is particularly appropriate here). That is, the first-person narrator can only see or hear or touch those areas his senses reveal. The first-person narrator can't, for instance, give us reactions to things he or she hasn't experienced because he or she wasn't around when they happened. So, using the first person must be balanced by the needs for telling the good story. If it can be revealed by keeping within the narrowness of the first person, that's fine. But if germane parts of the story remain elusive, then it's time to try a different approach.

That's where *third person* comes in. We call it "objective" in the sense that the reader is witnessing what is happening. "He," "She," They," "It" are how we characterize this point of view, and while it can't get as personal as first person, it has the advantage of allowing the writer greater landscape for story development.

> "The next day he decided to get in touch
> with one of the witnesses . . . "

Note how much more you can bring in here: while we write about his decision to interview witnesses, other characters could be plotting in other ways, and the prime actor wouldn't know of it. With first person we couldn't present those other scenes, but here we can. The writer is omniscient in the sense he or she can present various characters, unbeknownst to each other, doing a variety of things *at the same time*! Using the third person allows this, and the resulting mosaic could be more varied.

For the nonfiction writer understanding when and how to use these differing points of view is essential for good story development. Applying them in a dramatic manner has the effect of adding excitement to the story and creating an artistic effect. Philip Gerard, in his *Creative Nonfiction*, provides some guidance on developing characterization through point of view:

> "The first person narrator (the writer) can
> obviously let us in on the thoughts, fantasies,
> judgments, dreams, wishes etc [of the characters.]
> But if the writer does not want the feel of a
> first-person telling, it can be made to *seem* like an
> omniscient or a third-person limited point of view.
> That is, as readers we will get to know all the
> characters — or one character in particular . . . "

And once that character is deftly portrayed the reader identifies through the character's point of view and the story-line takes off.

A particularly strong dramatic effect with point of view is to shift it around, first one point of view . . . then another . . . then another, changing scenes and changing points of view. Fiction writers do this all the time; a novel may offer several points of view, each one providing a different perspective on the unfolding story. One of the more significant books that do this is William Faulkner's *As I Lay Dying*, written more than sixty years ago, it offers short scenes, sometimes only a page or two in length, and there are a number of points of view presented.

Nonfiction writers have learned to do this, as well. Look no further than Truman Capote in his classic, *In Cold Blood*, where the story shifts around from character to character, all offered in third person. Capote titled his book a "nonfiction novel," and that, of course, makes it less credible for the pure nonfiction writer. Yet, his story was certainly true and factual, and what he did was to utilize many fictional devices to tell the story . . . not the least of them presenting the story through several different "means of perception," and this is where his work gets very germane for us.

Because Capote not only jumped from point of view to point of view, he also made his jumps quickly, and in doing this he revved up the drama and provided an opportunity for other nonfiction writers to utilize this fiction-writer's device. It's similar to the story at the beginning of this portion where the professor had multiple things happening at the same time, and a sense of excitement permeated the classroom.

The same happens when we jump-shift our points of view, when we move from character to character, and we do it quickly. Suppose we're telling the story of a ballroom dance contest, and we want to get across the sense of excitement and competition and sheer tension. We could turn to narrative and write:

> "The dancers carried fixed smiles, and they
> were careful to maintain eye contact with
> their partners so the judges could see how
> merged they were. Shoulders held even,
> heads high, the couples never acknowledged
> one another as they twirled perilously close . . ."

We *might* be able to get a mental image of the event, but the sense of drama is certainly limited. The point of view was third-person objective, but without a change of pace or direction, the means of perception simply drones on and on. The point of view never changed, and this waters down the drama (though it could have been remedied if the underlying story had tension development of its own).

149

Note, however, the change we make when we shift the point of view and still keep the same story. Suppose we write:

"As the music began, Claudia couldn't help
remembering a night like this from three years
before when she and Jim had floated across the
floor . . .

Then, a few lines later, we shift the point of view, but not the scene:

"Devi knew this night was going to end
badly. His right knee ached from the old
cartilage damage, but he was damned if
he'd tell Helene. She'd decided they would
compete tonight, and that was that! . . .

And a few lines further on, we shift the point of view again, still retaining the same scene:

"Oswald loved these dance contests. He
rarely won, but he liked being around these
lithe, beautiful people because he could
sense which ones had the smugness
that made them vulnerable to his game . . .

Then, after a few more lines, we could shift back to the first point of view:

"Claudia was mildly jolted when Jim made his
waltz cross-over a beat early, and she had
to double-time to catch up. His eyes narrowed

and Claudia felt instant anger. It wasn't *her* fault . . ."

As we weave back and forth the level of tension in the room rises, not only between the individual partners, but in the room itself. Each point of view represents a distinct, abrupt change in the scene, and if the changes occur quickly, then the level of excitement rises because there's really no time to get settled. Bang! . . . bang! . . . bang! . . . change! . . . change! . . . change! . . . and the drama gets under our skin.

But to make this work we must remember a couple of things:

— changing the point of view should happen
   in short bursts — rarely more than a page in
   length before changing again
— it's better to use the active voice than
   the passive voice because we want to communicate
   that things are happening!
— be sure and return to each point of view so it
   doesn't seem like a throwaway device (which
   will undermine its usefulness)

Then, we also have to realize that shifting the point of view is a fiction writer's device for dramatic upgrade which nonfiction writers have adopted. This means that while the device is appropriate to any type of writing, the nonfiction writer must take care in using it to keep truth and accuracy paramount, writing only about what has happened!

But it still leaves a wide area of opportunity for the nonfiction writer. See, for example, *Old Friends,* by Tracy Kidder, the story of life in a Northampton, Massachusetts, nursing home as seen through the means of perception of several residents.

The nursing home had opened only a little more than a year previously, and according to the author: "It seemed so new a place for people so old . . . ." But gradually we begin to meet some of the residents and learn of their disabilities and their struggles. There's a fine line in characterizations like this because if the writer dwells too long on the health decline of one of the characters, the reader will grow weary because there's a sameness about the location,. *Everyone* has a problem of one sort or the other . . . otherwise, they wouldn't be there.

So the author turns to the shifting point-of-view device to build some excitement and drama in his story. And he does it by personalizing the story, offering individual points of view and shifting quickly.

page 101: "Dora sat in a rocking chair beside her window on Meadowview. She was short and stocky . . ."

page 102: "On her way through the lobby, Ruth ran into an old acquaintance named Jean Duncan. Ruth had taught Jean's daughters in high school . . ."

page 104: "There were two beds in the room. Earl sat on the edge of the bed nearer the door. He wore a nightshirt . . ."

Three consecutive scenes with three different characters or points of view coming at us. Little more than a page is taken up with each scene, yet we have moved around the nursing home and delved into the lives of three of the residents. Here is a classic example of shifting points of view developed to build drama and excitement. Suppose the author had stayed with one of the characters and instead of shifting about we had read three full pages of characterization, detailed and atomized for our inspection. Would that have provided *oomph* to the story? Would the sense of drama have been heightened?

Probably not, though we would certainly have obtained a thorough picture of the character, and in that detailed study perhaps we would have discerned something exciting. But the chances are more likely we would have come to *really* know the character and seek to identify with him or her rather than be bolstered by a rising level of excitement in the surrounding environment where that character may be playing only a partial role. In other words we — and the writer — need to be clear on what we expect the point of view to accomplish. If we're doing quick shifts, then we can't expect a thorough character-rinse; instead, we use less-developed characterization as a device to speed up the point-of-view shifts . . . and hence the drama and excitement.

On the other hand if we slow down the point-of-view shifts, extend their duration, perhaps even eliminate most of them, we can delve into characterization and provide a weightier portrait. It's not drama and excitement we're trying to build so much as it is substance, and here we have the luxury of time and space to do it.

But one of the hallmarks of the writing art is the ability to generate feeling and emotion, and dramatic impact certainly plays into that. I recall a well-known writer once remarking at a public lecture: "I don't care if you agree or disagree with me or even dislike what I write; the important thing is that I have moved you off a center of apathy. You have an opinion about my work, and that's really all any writer could hope for."

Art and drama go hand-in-hand, and where the writer can produce drama, some form of art will surely follow. Quick point-of-view shifts accomplish the drama part of the equation nicely; bang . . . bang . . . bang . . . things happen, first here, then there, then *there* . . . our heads figuratively swivel with each change, and as the storyline jumps about, we grow excited . . .

And we begin to feel something, and soon that something has grown and now we want to ride with it, and we sense the writer has built the world we've entered, and we want to find out what's going to happen next!

Such an approach works with stories of adventure and suspense. By their very nature these stories have a certain built-in level of tension, but quick point of view shifts can push that tension-level even higher. Any tale of true crime, for example, carries the essentials of conflict and drama in the basic storyline. Yet the writer may want to vary the tension level so the reader won't tend to grow bored or take things for granted. Changing the pace like this may also keep the reader's attention more focused.

The problem comes in if we overuse shifts in point of view instead of reserving them for selected moments. No one can sustain a high level of excitement indefinitely, and the accomplished writer knows when to turn it on and when to turn it off. Otherwise, after a number of pages, the reader's head could be spinning so much that interest just flags. But where the device is used sparingly, it will work well, and the drama level will rise accordingly. Nonfiction or fiction? It doesn't matter.

Take a look at Dan Kurzman's book, *Blood and Water*, about the Allies' rush to destroy the Nazi heavy-water facility in Norway during World War Two. He starts with a prologue that dramatizes the crash of a British aircraft in the Norwegian mountains in early 1942. Then, three pages later, he begins chapter one:

"Two months earlier, Brigadier General Leslie Groves
had apparently never heard of [the town near where
the plane crashed], a quaint, isolated, oversized
village darkly nestled amid snow-splashed
mountains about seventy-five miles west of Oslo . . . "

Kurzman spends the next five pages describing how
Groves and his scientists (at the Manhattan Project, the U.S.
program for development of the atomic bomb) viewed the
ominous prospects of German scientists and their heavy-
water experiments. He reviews Groves's character and offers
Groves's point of view for six pages. Then:

> page 11:   "When Groves took over as project chief
> [Leo] Szilard [Hungarian scientist], was
> working with Italian scientist Enrico Fermi
> on an atomic reactor."

And for the next page or so Kurzman gives us Szilard's character, offering the scientist's point of view on the work he was
doing. Then:

> page 12:   "The monster that would ultimately pursue
> Szilard was conceived during a moment of
> inspired reverie on a gloomy London day
> in September, 1933 . . . "

No longer Szilard's character but now his work:

> page 13:   "At this obscure but key moment in human
> history, Szilard suddenly perceived a way
> to make a chain reaction . . . "

For the next six pages Kurzman describes how the money was raised for Szilard's research and how President Franklin Roosevelt's agreement to fund the research was obtained. The shifts hereafter aren't as quick as they are in the early book-stages, but by the time page twenty rolls around Kurzman has established the higher level of excitement and drama, and now he can slow it down a bit as the entire story unfolds, and the succeeding points of view can be played out a bit more.

But note what he accomplished in the first twenty pages: he gave us characterization on Groves and Szilard, he offered three distinct points of view and he shifted between them, though he did not stop and start rapidly. He allowed several pages to elapse between shifts, and this works well when we're dealing with a couple of hundred pages or more; had the shifts come more rapidly — a page, perhaps two at most at a time — the higher level of excitement created simply wouldn't be sustainable. Eventually the reader would grow fatigued and lose interest.

Kurzman was wise enough to realize that his story, in and of itself, carried major tension and drama, so it wasn't necessary to become overly embroiled with tension-producing technique. Yet, short point-of-view shifts at the outset did rivet the reader's attention, and once that was gained, the book could proceed in more leisurely fashion.

Can we derive a general rule from all this? Perhaps in this way: the art of nonfiction lies in causing the reader to feel and become emotionally involved; to the extent quick point-of-view shifts can do this, the technique becomes one of the writer's — and the artist's — good and reliable friends.

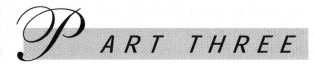

PART THREE

Literary
After-Effects

Literary After-Effects

———⚏———

One of the dilemmas facing any new writer is the urge to write a *good* book when the reality of eating has undeniable urgency, too . I use *good* in the literary sense, depicting something important, worthwhile and substantial, and I recognize its subjective nature; yet, all of us want to scroll our legends on ages-defying marble, and how better than by writing something people want to read for solid life lessons?

The young writer senses the opportunity, but there's the truism that few "good" books seem to find their way from best sellers list to classics honor roll. The young writer, of course, could be satisfied with the bundle of money when it rolls in; "good" has a way of fulfilling its own prophecy when affluence arrives.

Yet we run a risk when we pair material success with good literature because one may have nothing to do with the other. What makes a book "successful," at least in the material sense, may have to do with any number of factors unrelated to literary quality. Take the celebrity biographies and autobiographies: most are revelatory to the extent they feed voyeuristic needs in a prime-time audience, but they don't presume to offer more than a readable story with propriety's veil of propriety slightly askew.

But . . . material success may be clearly within reach, and the more shocking or frank the revelations the greater the bounty. To the young writer this might not only pass for "success" but as literary quality . . . when, of course, the two — at least in these instances — are mutually exclusive.

To be fair, that's not always the case, but we need to be assured the tail of material success doesn't wag the dog of literary quality. Certainly, if a "good" nonfiction book made its appearance, and it appealed to a large readership, the consequence of its possible material success should not be begrudged.

The Peter Mayle books about Provence are an example of this. The writing is image-provoking, the characterizations are formidable and the sense of place is vivid and sweetly drawn. He puts his readers in the heart of the country, and then he shows them why they should love it as he does. But it is the quality of his writing that allows us to feel these things, and once we sense his commitment to subject and characters we come to appreciate what he writes and how he writes. His work has become literature, *first*!

The question we all face is — when does a piece of writing acquire literary trappings and rise above the conventional stream? The issue is meaningful because literature and art are entwined so thoroughly, and if we seek to produce the one, we should be aware that the other must be served. For example, in the 1930s Ernest Hemingway wrote a nonfiction book, *The Green Hills of Africa*, a kind of travelogue and lengthy essay on camping and hunting and interacting with others through an extended trip in eastern Africa. He thought of his writing as nonfiction because what he wrote about, he claimed, actually happened, and he tried to present it in clearest terms. Here he is in the foreword to the book:

> "The writer has attempted to write an absolutely true book to see whether the shape of a country and the pattern of a month's action can, if truly presented, compete with a work of imagination . . . "

In other words, can a nonfiction work, utilizing dramatic technique, offer literary and artistic effects in the same way as a novel? Can they be cut from the same piece of cloth?

Unfortunately, Hemingway was before his time on this one because the 1930s critics weren't prepared for a departure from conventional fiction/nonfiction dichotomies (he utilized extended dialogue among other techniques). But Hemingway did understand that if a writer sought to produce "literature," artistic outcomes could ensue. The critics blasted him pretty thoroughly for trying to take conventional nonfiction out of its journalistic-based, fact-limiting cauldron, but he knew that for a work of nonfiction to "compete" with a work of fiction, there had to be dramatic overtones in the writing. He understood that the literary value of his book would be judged by its artistic rendering, and because the times were not ready for the "new journalism" which would arrive thirty years later, the idea of "art" in a nonfiction work like this was simply unthinkable and unsupportable.

Yet we look back now and realize that decades ago writers were seeking to develop art with their nonfiction literature and that when the break in tradition finally came — in the 1960s — novelists like Truman Capote, Norman Mailer and Isaac Bashevis Singer jumped aboard with alacrity. The nonfiction revolution was up and running!

But not all nonfiction is literary, in the same way that not all fiction is literary. We read popular fiction authors such as Danielle Steele or Sue Grafton or John Grisham, and we do get caught up in their stories, we find ourselves identifying with characters and breathless at some of the happenings. We learn — a bit — about esoteric matters such as crime investigation and lawyers' insecurities, but by and large it is the story we came for and it is the story we leave with.

Put it another way: we pick up Danielle, Sue and John because we want to be *entertained*, and they do that very well.

But literary quality?

For that we turn to fiction writers such as Susan Sontag or Philip Roth or Robert Stone. Sure, we'll gain knowledge about esoteric matters (read, for example, Robert Stone's *Outerbridge Crossing*, and learn what it's like to single-hand a sailboat across the ocean) and perhaps we'll also be entertained . . . but that's not the real value from the reading. What we get, more than anything else, is exposure to artistically written language offering unique and time-defying ideas.

In short, we get literature.

It's no different with nonfiction. There's literary nonfiction and there's something else. Both have a purpose, and both — as with fiction — have loyal followings.

But with literary nonfiction we get more than simple entertainment. Phyllis Frus, in her recent book, *The Politics and Poetics of Journalistic Narrative*, speaks of journalism as having literary value when:

> " . . . the text has either been designated a member
> of some literary genre such as the essay or satire,
> or has been labeled 'literary journalism' . . . "

And what constitutes 'literary journalism'?

" . . . when we read it for its formal beauty or
the universal truth it expresses after our interest
in its content has waned . . . "

Let's take beauty: here's Joan Didion in *Miami*, her dis-
section of Cuban Florida a generation after the Bay of Pigs disaster. She speaks of buildings which "seemed to swim free
against the sky" and "architecture which seemed to have
slipped its moorings . . . " She goes on:

"Surfaces were reflective, opalescent. Angles
were oblique, intersecting to disorienting effect.
The Arquitectonica office, which produced the
celebrated glass condominium on Brickell Avenue
with the fifty-foot cube cut from its center, the
frequently photographed 'sky patio' in which
there floated a palm tree, a Jacuzzi, and a lipstick-
red spiral staircase, accompanied its elevations
with crayon sketches, all moons and starry skies
and airborne maidens, as in a Chagall."

Note her image-producing adjectives: *reflective . . . opalescent . . . oblique . . . lipstick-red . . . crayon . . . starry . . . airborne . . .* all of these to call up a picture in the reader's mind.
But they also speak of beauty and it's the effective use of this
language — these adjectives with those nouns — that provide
a literary specialness.

At one level her book is straight journalism because she
investigates what is and was happening in a portion of the
country that seems foreign to many Americans. Fact-reporting

on the fears and the plotting and the hierarchical prejudices of this volatile minority would certainly be meaningful even without an injection of dramatic writing. But Didion is a novelist, and she brings her novelist's flair for drama to the scene, and the result is much, much more than an objective report on who, when, where, what and how events happen in Cuban Miami.

It is a complex picture of us and them, of historical animosities and imperialistic disdain, of local politics and national character, of pride and surrender. We learn as much or more about ourselves — we non-Cuban Americans — as we learn about the aspirations and the lives of the exiles.

For example, she relates that in 1980 a poll was taken in the Miami area of the "The Most Influential People in Dade [County] History," and not one Cuban name appeared even though fifty-six percent of the Miami population was of "Hispanic" — mostly Cuban — origin. She describes how Miami Anglos " . . . were in fact interested in Cubans only to the extent that they could cast them as aspiring immigrants . . . " When, for many of them, a return to their island home was what they lived for.

"There was," she writes, "in any such view of Miami Cubans an extraordinary element of condescension, and it was the very condescension shared by Miami Anglos, who were inclined to reduce the particular liveliness and sophistication of local Cuban life to a matter of shrines on the lawn and love potions in the *botanicas* . . . "

Here, she has given us a portrait of ourselves, and in so doing she has come up to the standard set by Phyllis Frus who spoke of literary journalism offering "formal beauty" (see above) and "universal truth." Is there any doubt that in this land where equality and non-discrimination play a resolute part in history and government and law, Didion portrays a portion of the population paying lip service?

Is this something we should know about ourselves? Is this a "universal truth"?

Is this the way we want our society to work?

And the answer — whatever answer we choose — becomes Phyllis Frus's "universal truth."

One of the most significant events in the make-over of nonfiction in the 1960s was the injection of "I" into what had been fact-based, objective reporting. Suddenly, the writer becomes a character in his or her own story, and the writer's reflections, dialogue and participation in events color what's written and even *how* it's written. As an example, take some of Hunter Thompson's 1970s work in his "Fear and Loathing . . . " series that appeared in the pages of *Rolling Stone Magazine*. Writing about the ubiquitous drug culture and its banal existence throughout the baby-boomer generation, Thompson explores the limits of that drug culture, not as a witness, *but as a participant*! A literary "You Are There! . . . and so is Hunter Thompson!" He uses dramatic techniques such as extended dialogue, flashbacks and vivid sense-of-place portrayals in order to hold the reader and give his story the necessary push. It was "new journalism" at a fever pitch because Thompson, unable to remain an observer, joined in the antics he wrote about, and offered us the "I" point of view. Here he is in *Fear and Loathing in Las Vegas,* cavorting with his drugged-up attorney as they "check out" the city. They are high on mescaline, drinking at the Merry-Go-Round Bar at Circus-Circus Hotel. The bar keeps revolving and the attorney won't leave until it stops . . . which it doesn't do. Finally, Thompson, who wants to get out of there, pushes the attorney off his bar stool and into a crowd of people, and they all fall to the floor. The attorney doesn't budge and Thompson walks out alone:

> "Did you see that?" [my attorney] said, as he
> caught up with me. "Some sonofabitch kicked me
> in the back."
> "Probably the bartender," I said. "he wanted to
> stomp you for what you said to the waitress."
> "Good *god*! Let's get out of here. Where's
> the elevator?"
> "Don't go *near* that elevator," I said. "That's
> just what they *want* us to do . . . trap us in a steel
> box and take us down to the basement." I looked
> over my shoulder, but nobody was following.
> "Don't run," I said. "They'd like an excuse to
> shoot us . . . "

There's no doubt writing like this makes for amusing read-ing, and most cataloguers would call it "nonfiction" because Thompson purports to describe actual events and conversa-tions even if he may have applied some dramatic license (in actuality, though, that's the basis of the nonfiction writing art — the careful use of dramatic license). But is it literature, and whether or not it is, can we feel comfortable these events actu-ally occurred as described? If not, then we're reading fiction; if so, is there some form of universal truth we can glean?

The literary question is the stickier issue because we're searching for art, and without literary effect, art will fade away. Hunter Thompson relied on his first person take for the story, but the story's basic effect is entertainment, and that, alone, doesn't give us literature. There's superficiality to this work, even if it's fun to read. He doesn't offer beautiful prose, and the only truths seem to be "free-spirited *us* v. up-tight *them*!"

Yet Thompson does provide something instructive: there's consequence, literary as well as non-literary, to using the "I" point of view, and we shouldn't overlook it. The journalistic "I" calls into question two things: the reporter's true, objective take on the "facts" as they occurred, and the reporter's influence on those events. With Edmund Morris's recent biography/memoir of Ronald Reagan, *Dutch*, some of this uncertainty is eliminated. Morris injected himself into the book, inventing a character with his own name and allowing that character to comment on Ronald Reagan and some of the events — and in this way he uses the journalistic "I." But at the outset Morris hints that he might get creative with circumstances: "The past is delusion, the future illusion," he writes. "One locates one's center where once can. Or, in cases like Reagan's, where one wishes."

At no time does Morris claim any influence over the events of Ronald Reagan's life. By his own admission, he's acting as a "projector"; his words project "a documentary movie about Ronald Reagan, which is absolutely authentic and thoroughly documented."

So the two major concerns about using the "I" in a work of literary journalism aren't present here (though other questions concerning the creation of imaginary characters in a biography certainly abound), and the result is a much more comprehensible depiction of the man. Universal truths regarding a man like Ronald Reagan in a position such as he held become more discernible as we seek to understand why he did what he did . . . and Morris gives clear, documented sources. Then, following on Phyllis Frus's thought that literary quality is found through the formal beauty in the prose, we turn to biographers Doris Kearns Goodwin and Michael Beschloss, both of whom, even with reservations about the fictional characters Morris created, called the work "dazzling." Goodwin, in fact, says, " . . . it was his [Morris's] technique to make an impressionistic version of Reagan, which is quite dazzling, the way it came out."

Clearly, then, we have literary quality here, even though the author has injected himself into what has hitherto been a staunchly defended objective preserve: the biography. It is the "new journalism" stepping over one more traditional fiction look-alike barrier.

But it doesn't mean the journalistic "I" has total clear sailing when literary quality is sought. Janet Malcolm calls it into question particularly when the writer has had an influence on the events. In *The Journalist and the Murderer,* her book on the relationship between writer Joe McGinniss and murder defendant Jeffrey MacDonald, she berates McGinniss for injecting himself into the story, then writing of befriending his subject and offering solace even while the murder trial was proceeding. In a final chapter, McGinniss provides his own take on the facts, concluding that MacDonald did in fact commit the crimes for which he was convicted. Clearly, she is bothered by the lengths to which McGinniss went to dramatize the story and by his crafty cultivation of a friendship so he could have the equivalent of a poker player's pat hand — *exclusive access!*

And then, when the need for the friendship has evaporated (because of MacDonald's conviction), McGinniss cuts his victim into pieces in order to provide a dynamic finale to his book.

Leaving aside Malcolm's concern for McGinniss's seeming disingenuousness, what she highlights is the inappropriate use of the journalistic "I," the injection of the author into the story and his participation in the events. "The writer of nonfiction," she insists, "is under contract to the reader to limit himself to events that actually occurred and to characters who have counterparts in real life, and he may not embellish the truth about these events or about these characters."

For her the journalistic "I," except in autobiography, is "almost pure invention . . . connected to the writer only in a tenuous way — the way, say that Superman is connected to Clark Kent." What she means is that once a nonfiction writer uses the journalistic "I," the validity of the observations, even the story itself, comes into question because the writer could assume a persona different (and less familiar to the reader) from the individual whose by-line graces the title page. Additionally, of course, the "I" character in the story — just as with Superman — might metamorphose into a more highly developed form in order to jazz up the story, and that means we're across the fiction/nonfiction line.

The crucial question, however, isn't whether we should use the journalistic "I" (because that question has been resolved for more than thirty years), but how it should be used. A large body of literature has been developed where the writer's participation in the story is, to use Edmund Morris's words, a "projector" for what is transpiring. Some of Tom Wolfe's early work, particularly his *Radical Chic* and *The Electric Kool-Aid Acid Test*, show this well. The writer describes what's happening, he provides extended dialogue, shifting points of view and quick scene cuts, and we have no doubt he's there, reporting it all . . . but he isn't influencing how things come out. He dramatizes the circumstances, to be sure, and he depicts cultural phenomena in ways that touch on literary quality. It isn't so much the beauty of his prose (though its uniqueness — as in his re-creation of sounds — can be captivating), it's the universality of the truths that emerge from his characterizations: the ultimate bureaucrat, the ultimate fawning snob, the ultimate poseur, the ultimate hippie and so forth. But at no time does he use "I" in the stylistic sense. We know he's in the scene because of the mannerisms and heavy dialogue he writes about, and that gives sufficient authenticity to the events. In Janet Malcolm's words, Clark Kent remains Clark Kent when Tom Wolfe writes.

There is one category of nonfiction where "I" is clearly appropriate, where nothing else would work, and that's with memoir. An excellent body of work has built up over time where memoir has achieved the level of literary quality: Walt Whitman's *Song of Myself*, Henry Adams's *The Education of Henry Adams* (which he wrote in the third person), William Styron's *Darkness Visible*, Tobias Wolff's *In Pharaoh's Army: Memoirs of the Lost War*, among others. The "I" quality of memoir is clearly its driving force because the writer is presenting himself/herself as *the story*. The writer is not only a character in the memoir but THE character, and everything that happens revolves about that fact. By necessity, of course, memoirs are written in the first person, the "I" person, because all reflections on events and other characters come from that point, and the vividness of the scenes, the personal nature of the experiences, are enhanced when the writer uses "I," "me," "my" and "our." It brings everything closer and that allows the reader to gain a clearer understanding.

The dramatic impact of memoir has grown in recent years as we seek to find out more about ourselves, to discover who we really are. Just as with the "new journalism," the 1960s spawned a generation obsessed with itself, what cultural viewers have called the "Me" generation. Naturally, writing about oneself, presenting one's story as more than a banal set of experiences fit quite well within the then-current context. Memoir developed into a form of role-modeling where the story became more than just a "good read." Now, we could actually learn some things; we could see, in their own words, where some memoirists went wrong and what they did to right themselves (if they ever did!), we could see into their hearts (because they opened them — boy, did they ever!) and let us know the nuts and bolts of their feelings and experiences. Writing in 1994, James Atlas remarked on our penchant for telling all:

> "In part, it reflects a phenomenon pervasive
> in our culture, people confessing in public to
> an audience of voyeurs . . . "

He cites the erosion of our notions of privacy and the self-actualizing urge to "come clean" as significant influences on what he terms our age of "literary confession." Memoirists, he says, have burgeoned in these times because our society reflects diversity and volatility, and " . . . literary narratives offer a substitute for the institutions — school, church, family — that once furnished us with a sense of personal identity." Memoirists tell us how and why, especially when we're unable to understand with the tools we've commonly used. We come to memoir for truth . . . or at least for one writer's take on truth, and in this we find the seeds of literature.

Because memoir can enlighten as well as entertain. For example, when we read Mary Karr's *The Liars' Club*, we come face to face with the hardscrabble life of growing up in a dusty, sweltering small Texas town, and we come to appreciate how the nature of the life colors the outlook of the child right into adulthood. Memoir that presents us with truths like this isn't simple confession; it's literary role-modeling. The point is that memoir done well carries literary quality, and tucked within its folds is the presence of art. James Atlas believes that even the novel has to share its stage with memoir now. "Fiction isn't delivering the news," he writes. "Memoir is. At its best, in the hands of a writer able to command the tools of the novelist — character, scene and plot — the memoir can achieve unmatchable depth and resonance."

Is there any doubt we're developing a story when we write, "Arising early Tuesday, I had no idea it would become the most awful day of my life . . . " or "What I loved best about Bear Island was the thickness of the trees that hid you so well you were invisible to everyone . . . " or "Mr. Dickens was a man of contradictions, thin as a pencil with a voice that boomed off the walls . . ."? But if all of this is nonfiction (and each of these is a true incident in my life!), how different is its *literary* effect from that achieved by fiction? The answer is . . . there's no difference because we're applying the same story-developing rules (foreshadowing, sense of place, characterization). So long as we're guided by the icons of literature: beauty of language and universal truths, the fact we're writing nonfiction, instead of fiction, doesn't matter at all. What's important is that we're writing it *well*!

We should remember that literary journalism is not a creature of the past few years. The idea that nonfiction in America could be literature dates back at least to Mark Twain in the nineteenth century and his letters and observations as he traveled. Here was no ordinary compilation of facts, but a story-teller delivering a story that, incidentally, also spoke of where he'd been and where he was going. He took the simplest form of communication — the letter — and made it a work of literature. Other familiar names, writing nonfiction — all with literary trapping — pass by: Oliver Wendell Holmes (the father), Lincoln Steffens, Sarah Orne Jewett, William Dean Howells, H.L. Mencken, Henry James . . . the list goes on. What's significant is that the literary nonfiction of today is not a thirty-year old orphan without connections to the art of the past. Where Henry James could write his nonfiction masterpiece, *The Art of Fiction,* in 1884, John Gardner could write *his* nonfiction masterpiece, *The Art of Fiction,* one hundred years later, and both offer a precise examination of what it takes to produce a work of literary consequence. Their nonfiction is literary (even though they examine fiction-writing technique) because they analyze and explain the nature of art and how it is achieved by the writer. Henry James would write:

"One can speak best from one's own taste, and
I may therefore venture to say that the air of reality
(solidity of specification) seems to me to be the
supreme virtue of a novel . . . "

John Gardner would write that the novelist:

"gives us such details about streets, stores, weather,
politics and concerns of Cleveland (or wherever the
setting is) and such details about the looks, gestures,
and experiences of his characters that we can't help
believing the story he tells us is true . . . "

Nonfiction, however, doesn't need to procure artistic flavor by attaching itself to fiction and fictional representation. It is an art form in and of itself, and what the writing since the 1960s has shown is how diverse and multi-formed it can be. Whether it's Tom Wolfe mimicking sounds to provide solid atmosphere or Norman Mailer, writing of himself but in the third person, and offering a memoir of war protest in *The Armies of the Night,* or Edmund Morris creating a fictional character for an authorized biography, or a twenty-five-year-old (Veronica Chambers, author of *Mama's Girl*) doing her "memoirs," the field is broad and filled with challenge. A book reviewer (Sven Birkerts) could extol his work "as an indispensable part of what might be called the 'conversation of culture,'" while Isabel Ziegler could write that one of the most popular nonfiction themes "is lifting the veil of mystery, going behind the scenes and observing how other people live, prevail and die." We know from Jessica Mitford's *The American Way of Death* how such an approach can develop into literature. Jessica Mitford's truths about how we treat death and dying are ages-old and modern at the same time. The universality of reactions from inside and outside the system, and her characterizations of them, are what gives her book its literary character.

But perhaps the most vivid example of effective literary nonfiction is one which tells its story simply and truthfully, without dramatic revving-up. In its starkness we can find art and literature together because the story is so compelling. This is John Hersey's *Hiroshima*, portions of which have been quoted earlier. Published, in 1946, a year after the bomb was dropped, the book made an immediate and profound impact world-wide. Hersey wrote with strict journalistic objectivity, never slipping into maudlinism or personal remorse. He collected the facts and arrayed them as if on a table, allowing the reader to choose which monstrous circumstances could be faced. He followed the lives of six people as they struggled to cope with the aftermath of the bomb, and he presents them without dramatic trappings, just tragic souls caught in the chaos and catastrophe. Here is unalloyed truth, so overwhelming in its pervasive misery and horror that drama seeps from even mundane observations. Consider:

"Wounded people supported maimed
people, disfigured families leaned together.
Many people were vomiting . . . "

Or this:

" Before long patients lay and crouched on
the floors of the wards and the laboratories
and all the other rooms, and in the corridors,
and on the stairs, and in the front hall . . . "

Because the devastation was something never before seen,
the details, themselves, were sufficiently dramatic for the facts
to stand by themselves. As Roger Angell stated fifty years after
the book appeared, "Nothing in the work has been dramatized
. . . " and in this simple judgment lies the genius of John Hersey
and the literary masterpiece he wrote. He didn't *need* to dramatize his story because the facts did it for him.

And these facts — these horror-evoking, painful, monstrous reminders — bring us to the level of art because they
offer universal truth regarding human survival : if we don't
control our tragic impulses, we have the means to destroy
everything.

In its simple, clear manner, literature like this — *nonfiction*
like this — takes its place alongside the great works of history.

Bibliography

~~~~~~

BOOKS

Burroway, Janet. *Writing Fiction.* HarperCollins, New York, 1996.

Frus, Phyllis. *The Politics and Poetics of Journalistic Narrative.* Cambridge University Press, Cambridge, UK, 1994.

Gerard, Philip. *Creative Nonfiction.* Story Press, Cincinnati, OH, 1996.

Jacobs, Hayes B. *Writing and Selling Nonfiction.* Writer's Digest Books, Cincinnati, OH, 1967.

Mettee, Stephen Blake, ed. *The Portable Writer's Conference.* Quill Driver Books, Fresno, CA, 1996.

Peterson, Franklynn and Turkel-Kesselman, Judi. *The Author's Handbook.* Prentice-Hall, Englewood Cliffs, NJ, 1982.

Rich, Carole. *Writing and Reporting News.* Wadsworth Inc., Belmont, CA, 1994.

Safire, William and Safire, Leonard, eds. *Good Advice on Writing.* Simon and Schuster, New York, 1992.

Sims, Norman, ed. *The Literary Journalists.* Ballantine Books, New York, 1984.

Sloane, William. *The Craft of Writing.* W.W. Norton & Co., New York, 1979.

Zinsser, William. *On Writing Well,* 5th ed., HarperCollins, New York, 1995.

ARTICLES

Atlas, James. "The Age of The Literary Memoir Is Now." *The New York Times Magazine,* May 12, 1996.

Berman, Rita. "Creative Nonfiction Writing." *The Writer,* December, 1997.

Birkets, Sven. "The Reviewer's Craft." *The Writer's Handbook,* The Writer Inc., Boston, MA, 1991.

Bodmer, Judy. "When You Write a Personal-Experience Article." *The Writer,* April, 1997.

Bosworth, Patricia. "The Mysterious Art of Biography." *The Writer's Handbook.* The Writer Inc., Boston, MA, 1991.

Bowman, Sally-Jo. "How to Write Irresistibly Delicious Nonfiction." *Writer's Digest,* November, 1990.

Braver, William. "Writing True-Life Crime." *The Writer's Handbook.* The Writer Inc., Boston, MA, 1991.

Callahan, Tom. "Writing Truth That's *Better* Than Fiction." *Writer's Digest,* February, 1993.

Fryxell, David. "Putting the Art in Articles." *Writer's Digest,* November, 1998.

Jordan, Eileen Herbert. "Writing the Personal Essay." *The Writer,* March, 1999.

Kirchner, Blanche. "How To Avoid Transition Trauma." *The Writer,* November, 1997.

Lenger, John. "The Key to Successful Personal Essays." *The Writer,* December, 1998.

Ramsland, Katherine. "Writing Biographies: The Problems and The Process." *The Writer's Handbook,* The Writer Inc., Boston, MA, 1991.

Writer's Digest. "Tell the Truth But Tell a *Story.*" Interview with John Barsness, June, 1991.

Index

Ackerman, Diane, and poetic technique, 7-8, 9
active/passive choice, 35-36
Adams, Henry, as memoirist, 170
American Way of Death, The, 48-49, 174
Anatomy of an Illness, 45-46
anecdote, and Jessica Mitford, 48-49; and Saul
   Bellow, 40-42; and Sally-Jo Bowman, 39-
   40; and Norman Cousins, 45-46; and the
   flashback, 46, 102-115; and Sebastian
   Junger, 44-45; as narrative device, 37-49;
   nonfiction, 37-49
Angell, Roger, and John Hersey, 175; turning
   mundane into art, 11-13
appeal to the senses, 20-21
Armies of the Night, 173-174
art, and nonfiction, 159-175
Art of Fiction, The, John Gardner's, 173
Art of Fiction, The, Henry James's, 173
art form, and nonfiction, 173-175
artistry, and broad appeal, 14-15
As I Lay Dying, and point of view, 148
Assassination on Embassy Row, 124-126
Atlas, James, and erosion of privacy, 171-172
Author's Handbook, The, 42-44
autobiography, and character development, 54;
   and quality v. success, 159-160

"Bandillero," 107-108

Barich, Bill, and use of inter-cutting, 126-129
Barsness, John, and use of inter-cutting, 121,
   122-123
beauty, in journalism, 163-165, 167-168; in
   writing, 8-10
Bellow, Saul, and the anecdote, 40-42; and use
   of flashback, 106-107
Berendt, John, *Midnight in the Garden of Good
   and Evil,* 62-63; and nonfiction technique,
   62-63
Berman, Rita, and appeal to senses, 139-140;
   and use of flashback, 103-104
Beschloss, Michael, on Edmund Morris, 167-
   168
biography, and character development, 54-63;
   and literary quality, 167-168; quality v. success, 159-160
Birkerts, Sven, as nonfiction exponent, 174
Blood and Water, and point of view, 154-156;
   and straight fact, 67-68
Boots, 20-21
Bosworth, Patricia, and biography, 55
Bowman, Sally-Jo, and the anecdote, 39-40
Browning, Elizabeth Barrett, and appeal to the
   senses, 20
Browning, Robert, 20
Burroway, Janet, and character development,
   52-53; and conflict as element, 27